YOU ARE ((NOT)) YOUR STREAM

CaseyScreamsBack

EDITED BY:
BENJAMIN SLEDGE

PRODUCED BY:

CONTENTS

Published by
HeartSupport, Inc.
411 West Monroe St., #28
Austin, TX 78704
info@heartsupport.com
www.heartsupport.com
twitch.tv/heartsupport

ISBN: 978-0-9991545-8-8

The information contained in this book is not designed to take the place of treatment deemed appropriate by a licensed clinical professional. It should be used as a self-help guide empowering the reader to better understand and communicate issues related to depression and mental health. If you are struggling with your mental health or have plans of suicide, you should immediately seek professional help. This book is intended to provide the reader with helpful information in the areas addressed in the book. The reader understands that the author and publisher are not rendering specific medical or mental health services or treatment. Readers should consult their own licensed professional for care and treatment of any diagnosis or condition specific to their situation. Therefore, the author and publisher disclaim all responsibility for any liability, loss, or risk, personal or otherwise, which may be incurred as a consequence indirectly or directly of the application or use of material contained in this book.

This publication contains the opinions, ideas, and personal experience of the author and contributors.

To every person who hits "Start Streaming." May you feel true love and care, whether with 0 viewers or 10,000.

FOREWORD

BY KITBOGA

"Are you sure you want to start the stream?"

"Nope, but for some reason—be it muscle memory or sheer accident—I've already clicked *yes*."

While thousands of bytes of data are being encoded and thrust across the internet, I've got thousands of reasons to keep my "starting soon" scene showing:

> Did I remember to get a drink?
> Is my hair looking good enough?
> Did I remember to update that scene?
> Is my title too wordy?
> I wonder if I should switch games.
> Is everyone going to like what I say today ... what *am* I going to say today?

When I first started my streaming journey, I thought I had most things figured out. I understood a lot of the technology side of things. Setting up a streaming computer and configuring the software wasn't too hard. I knew enough about audio to get by, even though I only had an old

USB Guitar Hero microphone that had to be filtered. I even had some friends that said they'd watch me if I started streaming.

What I didn't know was that nothing could have prepared me for the constant mind games and mental struggle that everyone in this industry battles with daily.

I had no idea what I was getting myself into.

No matter how many positive comments there are in the chat box, there is almost always something negative that catches my eye: **TruGamer69: ResidentSleeper this stream sucks**

You've gotta deal with everyday life battles like medical problems, financial stresses, and relationship issues—all while knowing later that night you have to somehow muster up the ability to smile and be entertaining. You should take time off, but you don't get paid vacation days. You have fears associated with becoming irrelevant or unpopular.

There is an onslaught of battles to be fought with ourselves as we play these mind games. As streamers, we are surrounded by people online but often we go to war completely alone.

When I met CaseyScreamsBack and his fellow streamer Danjo from HeartSupport over two years ago, I was so captivated by the words I heard coming out of their mouths: "You are not alone."

Maybe you've heard the saying, "Do as I say not as I do," used to speak of hypocrites and those who simply say good things without living them out. Well, these guys from HeartSupport are the real deal.

When I say real deal, I don't mean they're well-spoken professionals with fancy degrees. What I mean is they are incredible examples of what it means to care. These men, through their organization, selflessly invest their lives toward being there for people.

They're not simply saying, "You are not alone," and walking away. HeartSupport has built an entire community and arsenal of weaponry to support and come alongside and fight with you.

I have been in really tough situations where the HeartSupport team have seemingly dropped everything they were doing to spend a few minutes to listen to me and remind me that I'm not alone, that I'm significant, that I am loved.

My stream and online influence has grown well beyond what I thought possible over these past two years. I have the privilege of streaming to tens of thousands of people every day and gotten a unique inside look at what it's like to have what some may call success in the online world.

I still don't really know what I'm doing, and as I look around me, I don't think any of us do because there are tons of different ways to grow your viewership, plenty of ways to design your thumbnails for YouTube, and countless ideas about what game to play at what time.

I'm convinced that every single one of us is uniquely able to influence the world. No streamer is the same, no community alike, no genetic makeup a match. You are able to do things that no other person can do, because you are you. You're inevitably going to forge a path that is different than mine or that of any other content creator, but you don't have to do it alone.

Through success and failure, we all still feel defeated some days. We all cry at times, have weeks where we don't feel good enough, days we feel like we can't go live. This is only exacerbated by the negative comments, endless to-do lists, the feeling of constantly having to outdo our last stream, and the list is endless. The mental stress we all face speaks loudly into our lives, but HeartSupport is refusing to stay silent. They're right here yelling, "Hold fast, we believe in you."

This book, *You Are Not Your Stream*, may not have all the answers you're looking for and certainly doesn't have everything figured out, but it's an overflowing of love and support for content creators and people in new media. It's a practical guide on how to work toward figuring out the things you can and knowing how to be okay with the things you can't.

Think of CaseyScreamsBack and Danjo as the unnamed man in *The Legend of Zelda* who now hands you this book and simply says: "It's dangerous to go alone! Take this."

—Kitboga

INTRODUCTION

Hey, you beautiful human.

First, you're super brave. You just opened a book about mental health, and that can be scary. If you're nervous, remember you're welcome to read this book as slowly or as fast as you want. Plus, I believe if you put the work into the journaling sections and apply these concepts to your life, our Twitch community not only will be better broadcasters but we will also discover more joy and fulfillment. I'm excited for that possibility, but also excited *for* you. Writing this book has taught the team at HeartSupport a ton about streaming, self-confidence, and life.

But why a Twitch-focused book on mental health and well-being?

HeartSupport—the nonprofit organization that produced this workbook (and to which all proceeds go)—works directly in the hard rock and metal music industry providing fans the resources they need. Our founder, Jake Luhrs of the Grammy-nominated metal band August Burns Red, can tell you story after story of men and women begging him for help.

A lot of nonprofit social services and mental health entities have a tendency to raise awareness or give proceeds to mental health facilities. But what about the people looking for something now? What about those who could use a resource to reclaim their life? Jake stepped into that space with HeartSupport as the entity that creates workbooks, hosts live streams, and provides third-party counseling as opposed to deflecting to other sources. And if I've seen anything from the time I've spent streaming on Twitch, it's that even the best Twitch streamers need support—hence, this book.

The book isn't your typical self-help fix where I tell you you're a badass or order you to make your bed each day. Instead, this book is the result of countless hours of obsession, discussion, and frustration about life, live streaming, and my own mental health. Even though I'm the one writing most of the words, most of the content in this book stems from discussions—or rants—about the Twitch experience I've shared with my friend and fellow HeartSupport streamer, Danjo. This book isn't meant to be an end-all solution though. If nothing else, I hope it's a light in the dark when you feel like you can't see your hand in front of your face.

I've structured a lot of the content in this book around the most common responses we've heard from streamers. Our team at HeartSupport sent out a massive survey and gathered data from hundreds of broadcasters. We asked streamers what they think about themselves, their stream, the world, and their greatest hopes and fears. The following chapters are based heavily on the survey results, in addition to our own experience as a sounding board for broadcasters and viewers during the last four years.

If you're not yet convinced that even the most popular streamers struggle with negative thought patterns or that making it on Twitch is all sunshine and rainbows, here's a sampling of just a small fraction of the many survey responses:

> *I'm just another person on the internet. I'm nothing special. I have nothing to contribute to the bigger picture. It's already been done before (and surely better) so why bother?*
>
> *I'm in a big sea of other talented creators. Everyone else is "making it." I*

really have no place belonging in a community full of people much better than me.

I'm not strong enough. I'm not smart enough. I'm just not enough. I don't look good enough to be on screen. I'm not being helpful, funny, or entertaining enough.

I don't deserve all the amazing friends and viewers. Even though I should just be grateful, I worry I am wasting people's time that watch my stream.

I'm constantly worried that people think I am an awful content creator. I've been losing my mind, trying to get better. My window to improving is closing. The idea of not being good enough for others kind of haunts me. **constantly looking at the viewercounter**

Everyone says they love me, but do they really? Those people never show up. I have invested so much time and money. In the end I couldn't cut it. I will never get to where I wanna be.

It breaks my heart to hear these comments are a weekly (or daily) struggle for so many of my friends who stream. In fact, that's why we started streaming—to provide a place to find *live* encouragement. The stream was meant to support the community we had, but along the way, others joined us. We never imagined that four years later our stream would become the central hub of much of what we do. The viewers on our channel continually amaze us with their care, generosity, and hearts to help others. It's a humbling experience.

However, streamers can often pour everything into their communities without paying attention to taking care of themselves, and because of that, they spiral. Those earlier responses alone are a testament to that fact. Instead, we want those controlled by fear, lies, addiction, abuse, and destructive thoughts to realize their worth. We want them to receive help from their peers and provide the necessary resources to help them grow from a place of weakness into one of strength and resiliency.

If you're worried this book will include a lot of medical talk or mumbo jumbo that's too difficult to understand, that's not our style. I want to make this process simple and easy. No one on the HeartSupport team is a counselor or mental health professional. But we don't believe you need a degree to come alongside someone who's hurting and show them love and their inherent self-worth.

Twitch streamers are a unique blend of bravery, talent, and insecurity just like anyone else. They spend dozens of hours each week trying to brighten the days of others by broadcasting their lives. They put themselves outside of their comfort zone daily. It's inspiring. It's humbling. It can take a lot out of you too. And that's why we want to help, because *you* matter.

We hope moving forward that we'll help you not only have better broadcasts, but enjoy a better life. I can't guarantee you'll find everything you're looking for in this book. In fact, I expect somewhat of a Frankenstein mob to knock down my door and ask why I didn't include a chapter about something.

At the end of the day, I can only hope this book helps you think about yourself as a whole person who has the same fears and struggles as most everyone else. The things you're facing don't make you a freak— quite the opposite—*they make you normal.* Whether your stream is a nightmare, or you're just starting out, or you've been at this a while, above all, I want you to remember you're worth something simply because you have breath in your lungs.

Hold fast, Twitch fam.

CaseyScreamsBack

Chapter 1

STREAMING IS HARD

"WHY DO people keep posting that GreyFace? What's *that* about?" I asked when I first began streaming.

I would discover the smirking face was known as Kappa, which signifies *sarcasm* in Twitch emoji talk. But for me as a newbie, the language, culture, rules, and best practices aren't something you think about. Instead, there's a little fairy in your brain telling you it'll all work out, and hordes of adoring fans will attend your stream day one.

When my cohost Dan and I first joined the platform, we knew next to nothing. Streaming was one of those things we started without too much preparation or forethought. You know what I mean. Like putting an IKEA desk together at 2 a.m. when you have work at 6 that same morning. You'll quickly find yourself with odd pieces strewn about the floor, and you're convinced they threw them in the box just to jack with you. By 4 a.m. you're hangry and ready to throw the whole project into the dumpster and light it on fire. *That* kind of poor preparation.

Live streaming—we assumed—was a matter of turning on a camera, getting a decent mic, and making sure people could see whatever game we wanted to play. Three total ingredients. Sounds reasonable, right? But like most activities with three simple ingredients, you'll discover you need some different equipment, major help, and probably a good fire extinguisher.

LEROOYYYYYY JEEENNNKINNNNSSSS!!!!

Our first stream ever was a twelve-hour art stream for HeartSupport. We figured we'd do some drawing, chat with people, and have guests Skype in to crash our stream throughout the day. I borrowed a cheap webcam, got another camera from Best Buy, and bought an Elgato capture card for an HDMI feed showing Dan's drawing tablet. We didn't know what to do about microphones, so we just used a USB mic for Dan and a shotgun mic plugged into the computer jack for me. I loaded up OBS (Open Broadcaster Software) and assumed our setup was tight.

We had *no idea* what we were getting into. It was reminiscent of that old World of Warcraft meme where a group of players discusses a strategy, and another character gets fed up, yells, "Time's up! Let's do this!" and then screams his name—Leeroy Jenkins—as he leads them into certain death. Hilarious, on one hand. Getting slaughtered live? Not so much.

Because of HeartSupport's social media presence and community, we had a few people watch the stream—a miracle in itself. We didn't know it at the time, but it's common to have zero viewers for your first stream if you're not involved in a community or have Twitch connections. The bad part about having viewers on your first stream (and not knowing what you're doing) is that when stuff breaks, people notice.

> "Lots of echo on the mics."
> "Your camera's out of focus."
> "Music's too loud!"

Yeah. We had no idea why any of it was happening or how to fix the problems. Dan and I are both techies and work professionally in video production, but making a production happen live? Live broadcasting was a whole new beast.

Not to mention when we had guests Skype into the stream. Skype, for the record, was impossible to make show up in OBS. Or how do we capture a guest's audio? How loud do we make it? What is this dark magic?

During that first stream we scheduled rock stars to call into our super professional [insert Kappa emoji] production to discuss serious mental health topics, but our viewers couldn't hear them. And that was just on the technical side! We didn't consider the barrage of mental frustration that came with streaming.

> "What do I talk about?"
> "Why aren't more people watching?"
> "Was that funny or dumb?"
> "When is stream over?"
> "Why does my face look like that?"
> "Was that person nice or being a jerk?"
> "Am I nice or a jerk?"

And then the inevitable breakdown: "Everyone hates us and we suck."

When people unfamiliar with Twitch ask what it's like to run these live streams, after that first blunder, I describe the nightmare as follows:

> You're exposing the truest version of yourself to a bunch of random people on the internet and hope they think you're interesting. Mind you, this is all while juggling technical duties, fighting anxiety, and freaking reading tiny text for hours on end. The whole time you're kind of talking to yourself while alone in a room. Last I checked, this qualifies you as "batch crazy."

While streaming isn't rocket science and looks glamorous on screen, from the trenches it's dirty and frustrating and one of the most challenging/rewarding things you can do. You're forced to move way beyond your comfort zone, and the energy it takes to create content for people is demanding.

Dan and I have gleaned some wisdom from our streams after that first train wreck. You can learn a lot when you charge into a project like Leeroy Jenkins with your sword drawn and then get killed by a hundred dragon monsters. Failure will produce a lot of humility and an opportunity to grow if you let it.

But our experience isn't an anomaly because just about everyone we've spoken with has a hard time as a streamer. Whether it's balancing streaming with IRL (In Real Life) things, managing relationships with our communities, or tweaking our alert gifs until 3 a.m., many of us have the same basic goals when we step into the streaming arena:

- Goal #1: Be entertaining and meaningful with an actual audience.
- Goal #2: Don't explode into flames while chasing goal #1.

The problem is that it almost seems like the two goals are mutually exclusive. Often, chasing after the first goal of becoming an entertaining streamer with a powerful message can look like this:

If you want to make a big impact on Twitch, you gotta stream a lot. In order to have a respectable stream, then have the best camera, sound, graphics, and memes. Want an audience? Post to social media three times a day. How do you build relationships and connect with an audience? Let viewers into all aspects of your life and respond to direct messages 24/7. Oh, make sure you connect with other streamers. Look respectable. Buy the latest games. Create unique and engaging content for your social platforms. Don't miss a single stream or everyone will leave you. Why are your numbers down? Maybe you should do all the above more. Grind harder. Try harder. If you're tired, don't stop because everyone will leave you. Not working? Okay. Rebrand. Repeat into infinity. *Lerrroyyyyyyy Jenkiinnnnnsss.*

The aforementioned examples will turn you into a ball of stress and exhaustion. You'll end up holing up in your bedroom for weeks in a blanket fort, living off Uber Eats, and maxing out your credit card. If you chase the dragon without a good plan, it's only a matter of time before you end up like a car flipped upside down in Grand Theft Auto, doomed to catch fire and explode. But, hey, that's the life of a creative, right? We like to believe if we can land our dream stream, we'll finally feel fulfilled, until we experience reality.

The Grass Isn't So Green, Is It?

When I was in college, I daydreamed about the perfect job—what if I could just play video games for a living? I could wake up whenever I wanted, sit on the couch, play games all day, rake in the dough, and live a happy and fulfilled life! Life would be great. I'd write off my computer, game consoles—heck—even my couch. Soda too. I could freaking write off soda.

I'm sure you know the age-old saying, "The grass is always greener on the other side." I think it's something an old dude said to feel better about sucking at taking care of his lawn, but there's also truth in the statement. We often believe if things were just a little different, our lives would be awesome. Here's an example of what I mean. Have you thought or expressed similar sentiments about streaming?

> "If I can only reach affiliate status, my stream will explode!"
> "If I can get 500 followers, my stream will have amazing community!"
> "If I can get partnered, I could live off streaming!"
> "If streaming were my full-time job, life would be amazing!"

I've said all of those statements, not just thought them.

The hard truth, however, is that once you achieve any of those goals, you'll discover an entirely new category of challenges you didn't see coming. The grass doesn't look so green when the weeds wrap around your ankles. People within the Twitch community can start with all those goals in mind and accomplish them, only to discover the harsh reality of hitting landmarks and questioning if the work was worth it.

"I'm a Twitch affiliate, but there's only five people in my stream. Doesn't anyone want to watch me?"

"I reached 500 followers, but chat was dead during my celebration stream. Am I a loser?"

"I'm partnered, but I still don't have money rolling in. Am I a failure?"

"Streaming is my full-time job, but I feel like it's too much and want to quit. Am I stupid for trying?"

If you've reached a goal only to feel burned out and frustrated, you're not alone. Welcome to the club. We're all figuring out this crazy journey called life—and streaming it in the process—so things get complicated. And they get complicated because fun stuff is hard, and even dream jobs like streaming take a lot of work.

There's a myth that persists in our culture that if we do what we're most passionate about, life should be easy. You might have even heard this saying: find something you love to do, and you'll never have to work a day in your life. But that's a freaking lie. Nobody who's doing what they love as a job will tell you it's easy.

Passion is the gas that powers an engine, but the engine still has to do a bunch of work. If you believe that once you achieve milestones, you'll be content and live your dream life, I hate to break it to you: that's not gonna happen on Twitch or anywhere. Getting up every day and applying yourself to a task is a job in itself. It's hard, and no one gets a pass. If you want to accomplish anything in life—even something you're passionate about—you must put in the effort, sweat, and tears to make it happen.

The technical and practical side of streaming is difficult enough. As one person, you have to be a jack-of-all-trades. You need to have some basic knowledge of software, websites, cameras, audio, recording/broadcast formats, equipment, lighting, and social media. And this is all *after* you've gained some insight into what you want to stream, be it video games, art, music, crafts, or any other crazy stunt you can do on camera.

For the sake of argument, let's assume you're good at all the technical stuff for running a live stream and have enough experience to do it well consistently. Great. Next is the part where streaming gets crazy hard.

The Part Where Streaming Gets Crazy Hard

The biggest issue with streaming is also the one you hear the least about—the emotional side. This is the baggage that comes along with all the practical and technical side of streaming. It's not just a matter of turning on a camera; it's the frustration of troubleshooting a camera that doesn't work for three hours when you wanted a relaxing night. It's more than picking a game to play; it's weighing whether the game you're playing is engaging enough for your audience, let alone if the game is fun enough to play for hours on end.

Streaming is beyond setting up a Discord community. It's reading through a direct message attacking you for an offhand remark you made last week that made someone furious.

The emotional side of streaming is massive. All the baggage that comes with something that looks so simple and fun can be exhausting. When you strap into the emotional roller coaster, fear can leap into your throat, and you'll realize you're just one more person who has no idea what they're doing. You'll feel like an imposter, and the emotional hurdles alone can prove crippling.

No matter if you're a fresh-on-the-site baby streamer or managing a large audience, you'll face major emotional hurdles. We'll look at a few here quickly, but will discuss them in greater detail in future chapters.

The Emotional Hurdles of Streaming

#1—Self-Esteem

Is this your internal dialogue: *Am I good enough? Am I funny? Am I pretty? Do I have what it takes to do this?* Your own self-esteem will determine the way you act and what you do on stream. With little to no confidence, it's hard to do much of anything, *especially* stream.

#2—Intimidation

Twitch had 2.2 million content creators as of February 2018. The idea of going onto a platform where you're a small fish in a big pond competing for a piece can be intimidating. Many experience mental defeat before they even go live. *Why even try?* they believe. The hurdles get even more intimidating if you have a learning disability, mental health issue, weird mole, or anything that makes you less normal.

#3—Comparison

The comparison game is rigged, but we all play it. There's the constant pressure to be bigger than other streamers, and a constant frustration of having less. Even if it's not about numbers, we still envy looks, humor, equipment, donations, and life situations. You'll never win the game.

#4—Identity

Who are you? What makes you valuable? Are you a streamer? An artist? A content creator? Human? What you believe about yourself will define not only what you'll make, but how you live your life, how you spend your time, and what you care about.

#5—Creativity and Motivation

It's easier to lie in bed than to get up and make something. It's easier to hit the snooze button than to wake up and adult. It's safer to keep yourself locked away than to broadcast yourself for anyone to see. We have to make the choice every day to run away from what's easy and safe in order to stream.

#6—Content Esteem

Is what I want to stream original enough? With so many established streamers doing some flavor of what I want to do, why would anyone watch/support me? What makes my stream unique?

#7—Community

People are messy. Ironically, Twitch is a platform consisting of people who join like-minded communities, but where there's a community, there are problems. People will get mad at each other, spread joy, get hurt, need support, and be incredibly generous. Human beings can be vulnerable, beautiful, frustrating, and life-giving, all at once. And guess what? You're right in the middle of it because, as a streamer, you've built the community around your content and message.

#8—Fear of Failure

What if I put myself out there and nobody cares? What if I try my best and it's still not good enough? There's a nagging fear in the minds of every broadcaster they'll fail. We don't want to embarrass ourselves, and we certainly don't want to feel like a failure.

So What's the Plan?

You can think of a ton of reasons not to stream, and many I just listed, but hopefully you're still reading. If so, that means one thing—you want to overcome the hurdles and make something awesome anyway. If that's your plan, that's what will make you successful. A fast computer, beautiful emotes, or even purple hair (though it helps) won't make you succeed. The determining factor for whether or not you'll be a successful streamer is if you give up when times get hard. Or if you do give up, having the courage to wipe off the dirt and try again.

Perhaps you're already at the end of your rope. Maybe you've streamed for years and you feel you should throw in the towel. Or maybe you're just getting started on Twitch and you haven't even faced these struggles. You might be somewhere in the middle, grinding away and learning a little more each day. Either way, the goal of this book is to help you navigate these circumstances that will inevitably show up uninvited.

Together, we'll take a major look at all the emotional baggage that comes with building a community, creating content, and grinding on streams, while giving you tips to care for yourself and ensure you don't burst into flames. Throughout the process you'll discover new ways of looking at the world, yourself, Twitch—and even life.

Streaming won't always be as glorious as it appears, and it's deceptively hard to be a healthy broadcaster, but we're on this journey. So let's crush it. *Together.*

CHAPTER 1 JOURNALING
SECTION

1) WHAT ARE five expectations you had when you decided you wanted to stream? In what ways is broadcasting different from what you expected?

_____

_____

_____

_____

_____

_____

_____

_____

_____

_____

· · ·

2) What is the biggest challenge you face before hitting Start Streaming? Do you feel like that issue has gotten better or worse since you started? Why?

_____

_____

_____

_____

_____

_____

_____

_____

_____

_____

3) Rate your health as a broadcaster and creative in the following categories: 1 being the worst and 10 being outstanding. Briefly explain why below each category.

Physical Health: _____

Why?

_____

_____

Social Health: _____

Why?

_____

_____

Workload: _____
Why?

_____

_____

Self-Esteem: _____
Why?

_____

_____

Creativity and Motivation: _____
Why?

_____

_____

Chapter 2

YOU'RE STREAMING FOR A REASON

NOTHING HAS MADE me want to punch my family in the face harder than the original Xbox game Halo. It was the first game I fell in love with. I spent Christmas Day 2002 learning how to move around and aim a gun with two analog sticks on a frustratingly giant controller. During the weeks and months that followed, shooting my friends in the face with a sniper rifle over and over became an obsession.

In Halo, you play as an overpowered soldier of awesomeness named Master Chief. The premise of the game focuses on an evil race of aliens hell-bent on the destruction of human beings. When the aliens invade Master Chief's ship, it becomes your duty to safeguard military secrets and get off the ship, but not before crash landing on a huge ring-like space structure named Halo.

Events continue to deteriorate in your quest to defend humanity against the aliens as you learn the larger battle has just begun. Throughout the game, you have one mission: don't let the aliens kill everyone. That alone is your job. If you suck at everything else, you better not suck defending humanity. This sole purpose motivates your character and determines the course of action throughout the entire story.

We can learn an inherent life lesson from Halo and Master Chief despite the fictional premise—we have to know the main mission of whatever we do. That's how you aim for success.

We all have goals, especially in day-to-day life. For instance, if you text a friend about meeting later, it may be because you want to talk with them about the game last night. If you flip the Monopoly board out of frustration during a heated round, maybe your goal was to show that lousy, cheating family of yours who's right about Park Place. Sometimes the reason is less obvious.

Perhaps you said hello on a stream so that someone notices you, not just to greet the streamer. That party you went to? Did you go because it would be fun or to fit in and not feel alone? Whether we know it, everything we do has a goal or purpose behind it. Problems arise, however, when we don't know our goals. Think of it this way: if you don't know the goal of what you're doing, it's hard to know how to make it better. Even worse, a lack of clear direction could contribute to an outcome you don't want.

That said, if you don't know your goals for streaming, you won't know how or what to aim at. When you go about things that way, the aliens kill your face off. But before we figure out our stream goals, we need to do some groundwork reviewing our motivations behind streaming.

The Natural Benefits of Streaming

Why do you hit Start Streaming?

That may seem like an obvious question to some, but there's more to the question. Why on earth would you want to do something uncomfortable like streaming? Why invite a bunch of strangers into your life via a screen while they watch you complete normal human tasks?

More often than not, we start streaming because of a perceived benefit to our lives. While the benefits aren't the core motivations of a streamer, they do present some real opportunities when you're going live. The benefits alone won't answer the question, "Why do you stream?" but by looking at them, it'll help us get a little closer to that answer. Here are some reasons I like to stream:

Social creativity: Unrestricted, I jump into new creative endeavors daily. It's like an itch that needs to be scratched. Even just sitting still, I think of new things to create, and if I'm creating something, I feel happier. The reason—as far as I can tell—is because I find satisfaction in making something exist that never existed, thus feeling like I've contributed something to the world.

When I create, I feel needed in some small way. If people can see, hear, or experience something I've made that helps them feel joy, peace, or excitement, then I've helped someone. Creativity is my unique way of impacting this life. Even writing this book is an effort to make others' lives better and create an impact bigger than myself.

When streaming, I guess it's just a really cool flavor of creativity for me. Not only do I get to make content people enjoy, but they can hang out with me and enjoy the process of making it. Not only is it social, but creative. This is the real beauty of streaming on Twitch for me.

Technically, I could make videos in the traditional way: recording, editing, perfecting, uploading, repeating. But streaming is a much more organic and real process that fills a creative need within, while establishing common ground to interact with people I'd otherwise never meet.

I'm worth someone's time: Having people show up to my stream makes me feel worthy of their time. They like me enough to show up. The message conveyed is that I'm worthy of the effort it takes to log on and engage.

I learn about the world: Twitch has a wide audience. Everyone has different lives, different interests, and major differences in their personal philosophies. Streaming is a great way to experience a variety of cultures around a shared interest.

Streaming motivates me: Streaming allows two sources of motivation that are valuable. The first is accountability. If you have *any* viewers, they'll be expecting you to stream regularly. This alone—knowing that others expect you to stream—can be a huge motivator.

The second source of motivation is that streaming helps me with consistency. It's a well-known assumption that you should stream a couple of days a week if you expect your channel to grow. The more consistent the stream, the better. I have a hard time scheduling most things consistently, so streaming forces me to apply that discipline. When people count on you to show up on a regular basis, more often than not, you'll make it happen.

Discover Why You Stream

The benefits I just listed are good reasons to stream, but there's a major difference between a reason to do something and your core motivation. In his popular TED Talk, entrepreneur Simon Sinek makes a major point about what motivates customers to buy from any company. He states: "People don't buy what you do; they buy *why* you do it. If you talk about what you believe, you will attract those who believe what you believe."

The *why* is your deeper purpose behind any action you take. It's the layer underneath the benefits, the encouragement you may receive, and the obvious upsides to doing anything.

In the motion picture *Storks*, the main character, Junior, is a delivery stork on his way to the top management level of a shipping company. Junior dreams of running the entire corporation and is in line to become the CEO until he's roped into delivering a lost baby to its parents with the only human employee, Tulip. Throughout their adventure, Tulip hounds Junior with the question *why* he wants to be boss.

After traveling to the ends of the earth to bring a baby home to a new family, he discovers family is what he's wanted all along. Just like in the movie, too many of us assume we want recognition, fame, or money, when what we're looking for is a place to call home. In a fast-moving world of content creators all over the internet, we might think we want viewers, subscriptions, to make a living, a creative outlet, or any other item on a long list of benefits. However, where we feel most fulfilled is when we find the answer to our *why*.

You might think, "Great! Can you help me find my *why*?" but this is something we can't walk you through. It's a journey you have to take yourself, because it's different for each person. A likely starting point, though, is to continue asking, "Why do I want that?" Once you can drill it down to "I believe _____," then your *why* will begin to formulate. Don't worry! I'll give you an example so you can grasp this concept a little more clearly.

Here's what the *why* behind what we stream at HeartSupport looks like:

> Why do we want to stream? To encourage people.
> Why encourage people? Because they feel bad sometimes.
> Why does that matter? We don't want them to feel bad alone, thinking they don't matter.
> Why do we want to do that? We care about them.
> Why do we care about them? We believe they're valuable, no matter what.

Thus the key reason we stream at HeartSupport is because **we believe people are valuable, no matter what**. Your *why* is the driving factor behind your stream that everything's built on. Let's look at a related concept for a minute: success.

Define Success

Success is something that everyone chases. It's a word that has different meanings to different people. Success to a stockbroker might look different than success to an auto mechanic. Yet there's the seemingly arbitrary standard of "you made it!" that we all strive for.

How would you know if the auto mechanic was successful versus the stockbroker? If only money counts toward success, then you could argue the mechanic isn't successful, which we know isn't true. Thus, a big part of fostering good mental health for yourself and your stream is defining what success means *to you*. If you don't decide what success means to you, you'll always be wondering if you'll ever hit the mark. Shooting in the dark isn't just unproductive, it'll drive you crazy.

In order to define success, we need to figure out some major goals. These are the measurable indicators that tell us if we're on track or not. First, let's discuss some common goals—bad and good—we often see on Twitch.

Some Stream Goals That Are Generally Miserable

Number-based goals: If you're looking to land a certain number of followers, subscriptions, or viewers, I'm about to burst your bubble. You can't pick a number that will ever make you happy. If you don't hit it—which is likely as a young streamer—you'll feel like a failure. If you do hit it, you'll always worry about the numbers falling. And if you go past that number, you'll just want a bigger number after. This pursuit is anxiety at its finest.

Status-based goals: If your goal is to be a partnered streamer, you need to dig deeper. How does a Twitch partnership relate to your *why*? If you just want the status, you won't be happy with it. Even though there are perks to being a partnered broadcaster, you'll find out quickly that being a partner isn't everything and, as I mentioned before, doesn't guarantee revenue or an audience.

Financial goals: This is a big one. Twitch has a culture where a lot of money is thrown around. From subscriptions to bits to straight up donations, it's easy to see a popular streamer on the home page killing the game financially. The natural thought process that follows is that if you stream and gain a following, the money flows like the salmon of Capistrano. Yet, everyone will tell you, "Don't do it for money." But lots of people do it for money. So how are they still streaming? My guess is one or both reasons: (1) They're doing it for *more* than money; or (2) They're super miserable.

Some Major Goals That Are Awesome

Relationship-based goals: Streaming is about community for most people. Goals like making a new friend, brightening one person's day per stream, or sharing your story once a week with viewers may be helpful goals that bring you joy instead of misery.

Personal expression goals: These are goals that encourage structured time to relax, unwind, or care for yourself. If games are how you relax, a goal may be to play your favorite game three times a week. If you like to dance, but never take the time, a goal may be to dance on stream every Sunday at 8 p.m.

Creative or constructive goals: These goals include something you can accomplish on stream that is fulfilling. Examples include finishing a piece of art, beating a game, or learning to hit a milestone with a new skill. The point isn't necessarily to grow your stream but to improve your personal dedication and growth.

Your Major Goals Should Be Based on Your Why

Spoiler alert! If you're hitting goals, but not accomplishing your *why*, streaming won't be fulfilling and you might quit. The best thing you can do for your stream begins by setting goals that feed into your *why*. For example, if your *why* is "I believe service dogs help people with disabilities," then you might set a goal to talk about service dogs once per stream.

A longer-term goal could promote a local shelter or rescue program on stream; whereas, a short-term goal could be a doggy cam so people can see your service dog and ask you about the animal. Your *why* should motivate all major goals.

One of our goals on HeartSupport streams is to start meaningful conversations, and we aim for one major conversation per stream. Usually, we gauge this by discussing a post from our anonymous support forum (https://forum.heartsupport.com). Another goal we strive to achieve is for everyone to feel welcome. What this means is that if someone doesn't feel welcome, something needs to change.

We base both goals on the belief that everyone is valuable. We wouldn't want anyone to feel as if they don't matter. Instead, everyone who comes to a stream we want to engage, share their story, and believe we genuinely care.

Yeah, But Isn't Growth Important?

I'm sure our ideals sound nice on paper—Just focus on what makes you happy! Don't worry about numbers, money, status, or subs! Just have fun! But the reality is that numbers do matter. If you want your stream to grow, then you want your numbers to increase. If your plan is to earn enough to survive and break out of a job you hate, then you'll naturally care about subscriptions. There's no way around these realities.

So how do you balance the business side of Twitch with the warm, fuzzy side of what you believe?

What you'll need to decide is what you value as a streamer. While numbers are important, they're not the most important measurement you should define success by. An easy way to prioritize important goals is to do an internal audit. Get a piece of paper and write out your goals. Then ask yourself questions like, "If I only hit this goal and none of the others listed, how happy/fulfilled would I be on a scale of 1 to 10?" The numbers you write next to each will tell you where that goal should rank.

Chasing True Success

After you prioritize and write your goals, you'll see what determines success in your eyes. If you're hitting goals, it's safe to call your stream successful. If you're not, it's clear that changes need to happen. The reason it's important to define success and base the process off our *why* is because we'll discover what matters most on stream. This isn't just a useful productivity tool for stream growth, but it's an activity that's vital to our mental health.

Major anxiety, however, will come from shooting in the dark. You won't understand whether you're doing it right if you don't know what you're aiming for, and you'll wonder if streaming is worth your time if you don't have a gauge for success. That lack of vision will make it easy to cancel streams, flake on commitments, or quit altogether.

That may sound extreme, but at the first sign of trouble or pain, it'll be easier to quit than fight through. Even though streaming is supposed to be fun, the newness will wear off and disillusionment can creep in. We must set ourselves up for success to keep fighting when those hard times come, and the easiest way to accomplish that from the get-go is to define what's important from the very beginning.

While this simple step seems small, it's part of a bigger picture that allows you to actually be a healthy creator and not a burned-out one. Something as simple as writing your goals may seem absurd, but the clarity this activity will bring will help build a foundation for years to come. Just like Master Chief, don't go in guns blazing in the dark. Instead, get tactical and cap some alien bad guys to win the war.

CHAPTER 2 JOURNALING SECTION

1) WHAT ARE the top five benefits you get by streaming? Why is each one important to you?

_____

_____

_____

_____

_____

_____

_____

_____

_____

_____

. . .

2) Take some time to drill down to your *why* for your stream. What's the most basic, down-to-earth reason you want to broadcast? An easy way to help discover this is to continue asking, "Why does that matter?" for each reason until you can't seem to ask that question anymore.

---

3) What goals for creating and streaming have you chased in the past that have turned out to be empty?

_____

_____

_____

_____

_____

4) Write two to three solid goals for your stream that are based on your *why*.

_____

_____

_____

_____

_____

_____

_____

_____

_____

5) How will you measure the goals you've set to determine if you're successful or not?

_____

_____

_____

_____

_____

_____

_____

Chapter 3

YOU CAN'T DO IT ALL

"I don't even know where to start!"
"I feel like I'm drowning."

STAT: Almost one-third of broadcasters say they feel overwhelmed on a weekly basis.

WHEN I WAS in middle school, I tried to have a friend spend the night every weekend. Spending the night was—and is—the coolest type of play date. You can literally have fun until you fall over from exhaustion. There's no limit to the possibilities of fun when a stay-the-night party kicks off.

One particular summer evening I remember my friend AJ and I had all the fixins for a great time:

1 unopened 12-pack of Sunkist orange soda
1 bag of Nacho Cheesier and Cooler Ranch Doritos
1 Tony Hawk's Pro Skater 2 for PlayStation
2 top-quality razor scooters
1 full carton of Chipasaurus Rex ice cream
1 boom box with new batteries and a stack of CDs

Yet, as the evening faded, we sat upside down on the family room couch, bored out of our minds.

"What do you want to do?" AJ asked me.
"I dunno, dude." I shrugged. "Do you want to go outside?"
His indifferent "meh" said it all.

We had so much potential for fun but were utterly bored. *What gave? How could we be bored?* Looking back, I realize that the problem stemmed from having so much to do that we couldn't decide on a single thing. It's something the marketing nerds call overchoice or choice overload.

If presented with too many choices, people feel too stressed to pick one. This phenomenon happens on websites, in electronics stores, and even during our daily tasks. Many of us go through life in this constant state of feeling overwhelmed. It feels like there are too many tasks to accomplish, but not enough time. Then, when you add a time-intensive interest—like broadcasting—into the mix, it only makes our lives crazier! Over 30% of the streamers we surveyed reported feeling overwhelmed on a weekly basis.

Too Many Good Things

Have you ever sat down in front of your computer to work on stream stuff only to scroll Facebook for an hour? This happens to most of us. We often plan to work on something good, but because we don't have a clear plan, we get overwhelmed with the possibilities. The worst part about feeling overwhelmed isn't even the productivity aspect. It's the mental energy it takes to fight through the feeling.

When we feel overwhelmed, life becomes stressful. We fear making the wrong decision while time continues to elude us like a wanted criminal. Even in a relaxed environment, the pressure of choice overload can become so intense that it zaps our energy and is why so many men and women look for a quick escape. A quick escape provides the easiest way to relax, and the easiest way to relax is to zone out or find something to distract us. Facebook and social media have perfected a way for us to believe we're accomplishing something without doing anything productive at all.

If that's the case, then we're doomed to be overwhelmed, right? Even doing tasks to make our stream better would overwhelm us. We can connect with other streamers on Discord, make new graphics, update Twitch panels, revamp alerts, create another meme scene, find a new game to play on stream, adjust our lighting, find a new background, look at our stream stats, research chatbots, find better music for stream, create an outro scene, look for a better chair, update our wallpaper, adjust camera position, research new cameras, find better headphones—you get the gist. Thus, it's easy to see why all the work involved with streaming can turn into "Shawn just posted two more photos of his corgi puppies—cuuuuttttteeeee."

But here's the good news. The issue isn't that you have too much to do. Any streamer has multiple tasks they could be working on from dawn till dusk, but just because there's an endless task list doesn't mean you should do it all. The could-do items can be just about anything in the world. You could justify buying a huge donkey balloon as "I'm working on stream stuff" because "everyone likes big ol' balloons," but that doesn't mean it's what you should do on your stream. So how do you figure out what you *should* do? How do we find our way into clarity through the mountain of decision fatigue? Once again, it all comes back to your definition of success.

Goal-Based Tasking

Think through these questions for a moment.

- Why do you want to make a change to your stream?
- What will the change accomplish?
- Does the change push you closer to your actual goals, or is the change just something to do?
- If you plan to spend three hours revamping graphics, why? Is it better for your stream or is it just different?

We have to start with a major goal in mind. What would success look like for your stream? When we start with a goal, we can work backward and find what tasks are most important. Here's an example:

Stream Goal: For every stream, brighten one person's day by making them laugh.

Working backward to understand our goal, a way we've made someone laugh is by using silly memes on stream. If we want to reach that goal, then we should find a way to always have fresh memes. We could make this a reality by making new ones weekly and setting aside time each week to design them.

So a realistic goal might look like this: Make two new memes every Monday night. Looking at this process front to back, we can see that a solid use of our time would be to design funny memes every Monday night. Because this isn't just something we could do, we must make it vitally important to reach our stream goals. Discovering important tasks is level one of what I like to call Operation Focus Jackhammer.

However, this is also the point where things get a little scary. We can't do everything. We must cut out the less important tasks so we can focus on the very best ones to maximize our time and mental energy. This is the hardest part for anyone—streamer, writer, or even a businessperson. It can feel like chopping off a limb (yours, not a tree limb), and we're self-assured they're vital to success.

The busier you are, the more important we assume we are, and our culture reiterates that busyness = importance. Busyness isn't a badge of honor, though. It's certainly not unique to your circumstances either. Remember that big rambling list of options I laid out that streamers could do ranging from picking new chairs to changing graphics? Those are the same things any streamer could do, right? But there's no pride in being like everyone else. While you *could* do everything on that list, you don't need to, nor is it healthy to expect that you can.

Instead, be healthy. Give yourself permission to not do all the tasks. Pick one to three tasks you *should* do and let the other tasks sit on the back burner for now. You'll be plenty busy with the other items you need to accomplish. And guess what? If by some miracle you get that mega-list done, use your extra time to reprioritize the remaining stuff.

How to Crush What's Important by Focusing

Once we know what's best to work on, we can set a course to accomplish the tasks at hand. Consider this level two of Operation Focus Jackhammer. There's a wealth of blogs, YouTube videos, and books about how to focus, so I won't pretend to know the best answers. However, this is what's worked well for me.

1. Work on One Task at a Time

Every person tries to do this thing called multitasking, and it's a freaking lie. You can't do it. Do you actually think you can lurk on your favorite stream while updating your panels at the same time? Maybe. But it will also take four times as long. Plus, you'll be less engaged in the stream while remaining distracted from your work. If you want to get stuff done, do one thing at a time. It usually takes less time to do two tasks in order than both at once.

2. Schedule Time to Do Each Task

Here's another magic word we tell ourselves that's also a lie: *someday*. Someday you'll update your Twitch panels. No you freaking won't, and here's why. Someday isn't today, and never will be.

Instead, you need to say, "Friday, I'll update my panels." Guess what? Now you got yourself a plan. Even better, give yourself a time slot. The more specific you are, the better. For instance: "Friday night from 8 to 9 I'll update my panels." That's getting something done.

3. Cut Out Distractions

I love distractions. It's literally the point of the internet. Why else would there be so many cat videos? Have you seen the one where they throw cheese on a cat and the cat freezes up? Ha! Those videos are great. But everything has a time and place.

Cat videos are cute, but not while you're trying to get things done. Don't even think about opening YouTube while you're working. Don't have a ton of browser tabs open either. Turn off your notifications and, if you have to, put your phone in the other room. If you think of something important that you need to do, write it down, then work on it after you're done with your current task. Guard your attention like a mama bear guards her cubs.

4. Set Deadlines
If you don't have to get a project done, it can drag out forever. It's easy to justify distractions, to say yes to things we shouldn't, to break boundaries, and distract ourselves with other nonfocus-related items if we have forever to finish our projects.

A way to break that mindset is to set a deadline, even if just for yourself. Want more accountability? Tell a friend or significant other that you'll have a task done by the end of the week. Inform your stream you'll have it done by tomorrow. Put some deadlines out there, then stick to them.

5. Done Is Better Than Perfect
As much as we want things to be perfect, they never will be. Creative projects are especially imperfect because they're subjective. You can rework something eight thousand times and it'll still never feel done. In the same manner that we can't become perfect people, we can't make perfect things. That's why it's vital not to chase after perfection.

Instead, do the best job possible in a reasonable amount of time. A good way to measure how time intensive a project will take is to estimate how long it'll take and then double it. Realistically that will be the deadline. Make the best effort you can, but call it done before the deadline.

If you never finish something, then you can never move on to the next project. Also, that unfinished project doesn't exist in the world yet, because it's not done. It's a horrible feeling and super unproductive. This is also why so many fans are upset with *New York Times* best-selling author Patrick Rothfuss and his *Name of the Wind* fantasy series. Rothfuss has written each book already, but has continued to tinker for several years wanting them to be flawless, when that's not a reality.

As creatives, we have to finish our work. If you don't like it, note why, then learn from it, and do better next time.

Let's Taco 'bout TACOCAT

Staying focused is one of those adult responsibilities that sounds like a horrible drag to a creative person. When the word *focus* is mentioned, it almost feels like you're tightening the reins on the magical creativity unicorn that should be left free to frolic in the sunshine. However, staying focused will help that unicorn run faster and jump higher than ever before.

Because adulting words and topics sound immensely draining, I figured there should be a word that makes the process sound much more awesome. We'd need a word that covers tedious tasks like signing up for a Best Buy membership to get discounts and free money. Sure, you have to sign up, fill out the paperwork, and that takes time, but the rewards outweigh the paperwork.

An even better example is a driver's license. Learning to drive takes time, patience, lessons, and money. But after you snag that sweet plastic card of freedom, you can drive to Taco Bell whenever you want. And because everyone loves tacos, how about we call this new word *TACOCAT*? Even better is that it's a palindrome (spelled the same forward and backward) and will be our new acronym for describing this process.

TACOCAT: Totally **A**dult **C**oncept that **O**nly **C**reates **A**wesome **T**hings

Catching on yet? Focus is TACOCAT. Goals are TACOCAT. Self-care is also TACOCAT. Boundaries are TACOCAT. Don't fear the TACOCAT, even though he may look scary, because most of these adulty things aren't hard to do. They just need a little time and effort.

Plus, once completed, they make the rest of your life a lot easier. TACOCAT's a good fur baby. Scratch 'em under the chin, he likes it.

That's the important thing to remember about TACOCAT and adult concepts like focus. When you can focus, not only will tasks get accomplished, but you'll feel better about what you're doing. The most important thing to remember throughout this process, however, is why you're streaming.

Even if you're a casual streamer, it'll be a lot easier to feel good about your stream if your work is productive. This means you'll continue to look at streaming as a good thing in your life. That also means you'll probably keep doing it, which means you're 100% more likely to achieve your streaming goals, instead of burning out and quitting.

Before I close out this chapter, I need to discuss another aspect of focus I haven't talked about and that's control. You have to understand that not everything is under your control, even when you focus on results. This is a hard concept, but it's also freeing. Sure, you can control the content. You can control your schedule. You can control your actions and words. But here's what you can't control: if and when people show up to your stream.

Focusing on aspects you can't control is like chasing the wind, and you don't want to put anything on your list you can't control. You'll never be able to control whether people like you, whether they send a raid, donate, cheer with bits, or even post messages in the chat. Yes, you can do things to influence a viewer's behavior and make efforts to network better, but it's up to the viewer to decide how they'll respond.

If you want to stay sane and be a healthy streamer, focus on the most important things you *can* control. Because when we focus on goals as broadcasters, it's easier to see the road laid out before us, and all we need to do is keep driving.

CHAPTER 3 JOURNALING SECTION

1) WRITE a list of all the tasks you want to do to work on your stream. How many of them push you closer to your goals you set earlier? Cross out the ones that don't contribute directly to your goals.

_____

_____

_____

_____

_____

_____

_____

_____

_____

_____

. . .

2) Now pick the three most important from the list of goals and schedule a time on a weekly basis to work on them.

Goal 1 _____

_____

I'll work on this for _____ minutes on this day: _____

Goal 2 _____

_____

I'll work on this for _____ minutes on this day: _____

Goal 3 _____

_____

I'll work on this for _____ minutes on this day: _____

3) Which aspects of your stream/workload are out of your control? Name one thing you need to let go of to stay focused and be more productive.

_____

_____

_____

_____

Chapter 4

YOU WILL NEVER BE "ENOUGH"

My buddy grabs my shoulder as I gaze at the flashing lights in the arcade and states, "I will drag you out of here if you play it again."

We're at a place in town called Putters. It's one of those family-fun places with mini-golf, video games, pizza, and laser tag. In middle school, it was what the kids referred to as "the bee's knees." The pizza is gross and overpriced, the golf course is boring, and unexplained stickiness covers the laser tag arena, but the place is dope. Within this glowing gem of childhood dreams stands a certain game that strikes fear and worry into the hearts of those I love.

The game in question is a huge plastic piano, and the objective is to hit the correct keys as fast as you can. The more you hit, the higher the score. Beat doesn't matter, and tempo doesn't matter. The musical side of me has a fit, but the side of me that likes a challenge can't get enough of this thing. The highest score you can get is 99, and I only know this because that's what I'm after every time I grace the arcade.

I've set the high score too many times to count, but always come back for more. Do I keep playing to defend my record? Not really. They reset the scores every day. I also know there are a few other people who can hit 99 easily, so their names go up on the scoreboard. But every time I'm there, I'm after that 99. You'd think once I hit the high score

I'd be done, right? Wrong. I have to hit it twice. Three times. I play until I'm out of money. The real reason I keep playing is because no matter how well I do, I always believe I can one-up myself. It's a bad deal all around. These days, I'm encouraged not to play the piano game.

Falling Short

As broadcasters, it's easy to browse through channels on Twitch and look at streams with the stunning graphics, professional lighting, and tons of subscribers, only to conclude our stream isn't enough. We assume everyone else has it together and we'll never hit the same level of success. It's not just about what our stream looks like or how it performs, but about the constant nagging suspicion that we're not where we should be in life. We conclude we don't measure up at the moment, so we better keep pushing. Just like my playing that addictive piano game, we tell ourselves over and over we can do better. We can hit 99.

The negative self-spiral can start with a small thought at the worst time. Perhaps you had a rough day before stream. Your eyes are puffy from allergies, and you didn't get enough sleep the night before. Once you fire up your computer, you discover your webcam isn't working—again. So you spend twenty minutes troubleshooting it only to find it got unplugged last night so Travis could charge his vape pen. "Stupid Travis thinks he can just do whatever he wants!" You huff. "How 'bout he charges a punch to the face?"

So you start up stream twenty minutes late, exhausted and still pissed at Travis, itching your eyes, and wondering why that Chevy Blazer cut you off in traffic. A few minutes into stream, a new viewer pops on and says something like, "Yo, you look like you need some sleep, babe." *I need some sleep? How about coming to your apartment, kick in the door, and toss you into the sun? That's what I need right now.*

While being mad is fun, it doesn't solve the problem. The real issue is that, deep down, you know he's right. We tend to get most angry when we're at the end of our rope and feeling a little sensitive. It's not even that we may look a little tired, because that's true for everyone at times. It's the deeper belief whispering to us that we try to ignore.

The part bothering us is that subconsciously we might decide we aren't pretty or handsome enough. We don't have big enough eyes or smooth enough skin. We're terrified we're not attractive, worthwhile, or interesting and believe people can see right through us. Soon enough, they'll figure out we're not worthy enough to care for. We're scared viewers will come onto our stream and decide our value for us.

The Most Dangerous Word I Know

When I was seven, I decided the most dangerous thing in the universe had to be burrowing electric flying monster spiders. These monsters can climb, fly, and dig, so there's no escaping them. If you jumped into a lake to escape their wrath, they'd just electrocute you. Even their poison fangs shock you when they bite. You also have to deal with the fact that the spiders travel in large groups so you can't kill all of them, if confronted. Let's face it, if you encountered a pack of these things in the wild, you're doomed.

Lucky for you and me, however, burrowing electric flying monster spiders aren't real (to my knowledge), so we'll be okay. Yet, I've found something that exists in our language just as dangerous as these imaginary monsters—the word *enough.*

Enough is a killer for a couple reasons. The first being that the concept isn't fully based on facts. In school, there's a clear standard on standardized tests. An average of 70% or more is the defining factor that determines whether you answered enough questions correctly. In life, however, there's almost never a clear standard for what enough is.

You can ask ten different people what it means to be responsible enough and get ten different answers. The irony is that we assign some kind of arbitrary standard to whatever we're feeling sensitive to in the moment, then chase after said standard like our life depends on it.

Each person has a different area where they feel they're falling short and can appear in a variety of manners—not attractive enough, strong enough, funny enough, or outgoing enough. Whereas one person may struggle with their appearance, another may not. But they may struggle with being productive enough. Here's where it gets interesting though. Even in those individual categories, none of us can seem to put our finger on what enough really is.

It gets deadly when we apply a random standard to what we deem enough. This imaginary standard is most often beyond where we currently are. You may have lost ten pounds this month, but still don't feel skinny enough. Perhaps you hit a hundred viewers the other day, but the number didn't feel as good as expected, so maybe one hundred and fifty will be enough. Many people believe once they hit goals, their life will achieve some semblance of comfort, meaning, or purpose. Yet, when we hit those numbers, the achievement still doesn't give us the satisfaction we were seeking, and we move our standard higher.

No one has made this more plain than New England Patriots' quarterback Tom Brady. In an interview with *60 Minutes*, he said:

> There're times where I'm not the person that I want to be. Why do I have three Super Bowl rings and still think there's something greater out there for me? I mean, maybe a lot of people would say, "Hey man, this is what it is." I reached my goal, my dream, my life. Me, I think: God, it's gotta be more than this. I mean this can't be what it's all cracked up to be. I mean I've done it. I'm twenty-seven. And what else is there for me?

Most people would kill to have Tom Brady's life and success, and yet when he's arrived, he discovers the same discontentment other people feel when they tackle goals on stream. Our own standards are an ever-increasing bar we never seem to reach, just like the piano game at the arcade. So how do we combat that?

Redefine Our Enoughs

One of the biggest ways to fight not being enough is to accept where we are now. The way we define *enough* currently in our culture is with an arbitrary and ever-moving standard that we'll never reach, right? Shame researcher Brené Brown points out that courage, compassion, and connections with other people are the keys to a wholehearted life. When we emulate those traits, they help us belong and feel enough, but it's up to each one of us to reframe our *enoughs*.

Being enough can't be based on some future goal or achievement because, as I stated, that bar keeps moving further away. You must accept today that you're worthy of love and belonging solely because of who you are.

For some people (like me), that can be because a higher power believes you're worthy of love. For others, that can be a deep indwelling knowledge of familial love and friendships that helps define your worthiness. Even if you have only one friend, that one friend believes you are worthy enough because they chose you as a friend after all. Who cares if you're not x-number of steps beyond where you are right now? You're exactly in the position you're at in life for the moment and not beyond it. To expect yourself to be beyond where you're at now is like beating yourself up because you don't have three arms and haven't figured out time travel. It makes no sense.

We need to shift our definition from an unattainable standard to a realistic expectation that's grounded in things that matter. You'll never be pretty enough because someone out there will always be more attractive. Plus, how people view beauty is subjective. But you can shower and wash your hair because you're worthy of respect. You can do your nails because it's fun. You can wear your favorite shirt because it's softer than a puppy. You can put effort into your appearance to show your viewers you care.

You'll always feel as if you can do something better, but that's okay. From grocery clerks to celebrities and everyone in between, we're all floating in the same boat. If you find yourself craving a certain status or achievement, it's important to ask a deeper question: What about this will fulfill me? Do you want to be as popular as Ninja on Twitch? Why? So that people will love and respect you? Will you then feel you have worth? Why do you want to be a Twitch Partner? Is it so your hard work becomes validated?

By examining those deeply held desires, you might just recognize that your definition of enough isn't really about the achievement, but more about the feelings you assume come with success. Chasing any achievement without self-worth is useless, because it's like building a house without a foundation. You have to first believe you're worthy of love. As Brené Brown says, "Believing that you're enough is what gives you the courage to be authentic, vulnerable, and imperfect."

You may say, "This sounds good and all, but how do I start to believe I'm enough right now?" Great question.

Begin by surrounding yourself with safe people who encourage you. We're not supposed to do life alone, but it's easier than ever to miss real connection and solely plug our emotions in social media. Instead, find a trusted friend or group of friends that can call you out when you're being too hard on yourself. It's easy to get stuck inside your head and become convinced you're terrible and life will never get better. Moreover, you buy into the belief that no one else in the world struggles with the same emotions and hardships.

Having a group of people around you allows people to say, "Hey, you're trying to be enough again. I did that yesterday. Let's remember that we're both awesome." Also, redefine what *enough* means to you. Stop defaulting to the assumption you're not good enough. Talk about it. Write about it. Figure out where a realistic standard lives. Bounce your new standards off that group of safe, encouraging people. Let them ask you hard questions and be honest. Being honest about what you're experiencing can be terrifying, but remind yourself that vulnerability is where you'll find true acceptance and, with that, worthiness.

A Stream That's Enough

Imagine if people on Twitch began living like they're worthy? What if we chased after what matters as opposed to cutting ourselves short and focusing on imperfections and where we fall short? Not only would we have better streamers but healthier viewers who can begin to believe they, too, are enough. Think about what your next stream would be like if you choose confidence over fear? How much easier would it be to ignore the trolls if you felt good about how you look now? How much more fun would that game be if you weren't cutting yourself down every second?

I'll be the first to admit I'm not great at executing these concepts, but in the times where I realize I don't have to live in a state of disappointment because I'm not further along, I relax. When we give ourselves the grace we deserve, we can focus on being the most authentic version of ourselves as opposed to wishing we were someone else further along. Maybe then we'll have more fun and enjoy our streams in the way we've always wanted.

You Don't Have to Be the Best

In my hometown there's a dance school. It's an amazing place where young people can learn a variety of dance styles and perform regularly. Not only do students learn how to be better dancers, but they learn about self-image and hard work, all while encouraging each other to be bolder and better people.

The school is a magnificent place, and one long-term student in particular has shown continued talent. For the sake of anonymity, I'll call her Leigh. When I went to a recent dance recital, Leigh was easy to spot from a distance. I know little about dance, but I could see how much she cared about doing a good job. Her moves were deliberate and her stage presence brimmed with energy.

If you planned to pick the top five most impressive dancers in the studio, she would be in the batch. As I watched her dance with the team, I wondered what it would be like to be the dancer next to Leigh. *What would I be thinking? Would I second-guess each move? Would I resent her because of her natural skill?* Perhaps I might even be frustrated that she appears to have it all.

But as an outsider looking in, I didn't feel any of those emotions. As an audience member, there was no need to be jealous. Sitting there in my seat, I didn't conclude I was any worse or less important than she was. There wasn't the slightest hint of bitterness about how well she moved compared to how I move.

The reason I didn't feel threatened was because I'm not a dancer. It's easy to say "that guy's a great pilot" if you never fly planes. It's not a big deal to exclaim "wow, what an amazing artist" if you don't draw. Because we don't do comparable activities, that makes it okay to give someone a compliment with no thought of competition. What does it matter if someone is adept at a skill you don't care about?

But if your skill set *is* in the same genre, that's where pride kicks in. Instead of simple admiration, the dreadful beasts of comparison, greed, and jealousy rear their ugly heads. We compare apples to apples—as the saying goes—to judge who is better or more skilled or talented. For instance, if you're an artist, you can put a drawing next to a competitor's and vote on the winner. If you're a singer, simply compare recordings with any other singer. If there's an inadequacy there, then our emotions boil over.

If our talents are in the same genre as another person, we assume there's an ongoing competition. Each of us knows what that competition feels like too. Any time the other person does something amazing, you feel the need to step up your game. You're happy when you win, and happy when they fall. If they're having a bad day, your day gets a little brighter; whereas, if you were having a bad day, you'd be frustrated or resentful of their success. It's interesting, isn't it, that in competition it seems okay to rejoice in someone else's misfortune?

Context, though, is the key. I'm not condemning competition, as it's a healthy outlet at times. When we join a game, race, or contest, we accept the terms of the competition. We agree—at least on the surface —that it's just a game. There will be a winner and a loser, and sometimes the outcome is brutal.

Boxing is a perfect example of brutal terms in a competition. If two people sign up for a boxing match, both agree to get punched in the face. Someone goes home the loser, and there's no trophy or potential earnings. However, the winner is congratulated for punching someone in the face.

In normal day-to-day life, by comparison, if you deck some dude in the face, you usually get a ride in a police car. Thus, competition is considered in a specific context. People agree to follow the rules of the game and understand that there can only be one winner. Yet, it's envy that brings a competitive nature into a noncompetitive context. That's the point here. Just because you're doing the same thing as someone else does not mean you're competing with them. Instead, that unhealthy competitiveness is often self-induced.

Easy Answers to Complex Questions

Why do we compare and compete in activities that shouldn't be competitions? Have you ever wondered that? Why do we strive so hard to be better than other people when they may have done nothing to us?

Going back to the last chapter's theme, I suspect it comes back to these questions: Do I matter? and Am I good enough? Insecurities fester when we have someone to compare ourselves to. We look for an easy yes or no answer to the questions of purpose and importance and then set up arbitrary standards to give us an answer. For instance, if I were in the same dance class as Leigh, my subconscious thought process might go something like this: if I can dance better than Leigh, then I'm good enough. If she doesn't miss a step, but I do, then I should quit because I'm not as talented.

Our psyche tries to find quick and easy answers to complex questions of meaning and purpose in life. But it never answers the real question we're after. Instead, we get a marker to point out we're at least better than someone else. But comparison is a killer that will eat us alive and do anything but give us purpose and meaning.

Dwell on this question for a minute: When was the last time you felt discouraged about your stream and why? Was it because you legitimately had a terrible time and there were numerous technical problems? Or was it because you looked at someone else's stream and thought, *I'll never have a stream like that?* I'm not casting shade at you if you have, because I've done it too.

On my personal music stream I do a variety of vocal performances, recording, and mixing. I like my stream. I even have dedicated viewers who love showing up—Every. Single. Time. Yet, I've often browsed through the music category on Twitch to find yet another pretty girl playing that same stupid song for hundreds of viewers. That's when my pride and jealousy took over, and I spiraled.

I say to myself, *She's not even that great of a singer. Anyone can do that. She cheated the system. She plays the same ten songs, every stream! Why do people even show up?* At once I felt frustration, bitterness, and self-righteousness in one crazy jealousy-ball. Even my good-natured bent toward that streamer dwindled because I felt threatened that streamers like her will take all the other viewers—with their so-called less interesting content—and I'll be left to chase scraps. On top of everything else I'm processing, I fear I won't ever have a stream as awesome.

It's hard to keep going when you feel you'll never be as good as the people you admire. It's far easier to just hate them and quit. Thus, when you review the answer to the question, Do I matter? in that light, the subsequent response crushes you: *I don't matter because that streamer will always be better than I am. She'll always have bigger numbers, better content, and awesome hair. I should quit before wasting more of my time.*

What's interesting about this thought process is that I'm sure there are people thinking the same thing about my stream. I'm willing to bet there's someone browsing through Twitch who stopped and lurked for a few moments, only to realize that I have twice their viewership, I appear to wear nicer clothes, and then conclude my content sucks. But this spiral isn't just for me or other lower-level streamers. While I might have been jealous of that female streamer, she might feel envious or even hate another streamer.

The broadcaster with thousands of viewers can stay up all night wondering why they don't have tens of thousands like that jerk they saw on the front page of Twitch. There will always be bigger fish, and we can't base our worth on whether we're the best because we'll never get there. Even if we did, it'd be a short run until we're second best once more.

Even in a competitive context with winners and losers, tying our value to how our talents compare to others isn't healthy. Yet it's far worse amid activities that aren't a competition. Especially in life, streaming, and normal creative outlets. We feel threatened and envy others because of their talents, audience, content, or humor, even though we're not in competition with them. When it becomes a competition, your proverbial well is no longer safe. It's poisoned. Because streaming isn't a contest.

Streaming Isn't a Contest

Broadcasters tell themselves a powerful lie. The lie is that there won't be enough views to go around. We feel like it's our mission to take views away from other channels so we can be the best, and then we get defensive when other channels seem to do the same to our stream. It's as if we believe people who watch Twitch are some kind of limited resource—much like the last cinnamon roll at Grandma's.

For the sake of argument, I guess—technically—the number of viewers on Twitch is finite. But that number is so far beyond what any one channel can handle, it's not relevant. This mentality is like going to the ocean and getting mad at a kid filling up a bucket with water because there isn't enough to go around. While the amount of water in the ocean is limited, there's no way one kid will ruin it for the rest of us. We treat that streamer who is apparently "taking all my views" in the same manner. If they go offline, chances are it won't make much of a difference toward our viewership, so we all need to calm down.

Another important reminder in our modern age is that most people have multiple browser tabs open on their computer. What this means is that streams aren't even exclusive either. A viewer can lurk in two or three streams at a time with little trouble, so that's just another nail in the coffin for the "they're taking my views" argument. In reality, what makes or breaks your stream isn't the game you play, the transitions, the memes, the graphics, or the viewership. *It's you.* You are the reason you have a stream. You are the reason any viewers show up. And in all the history of the entire planet, there will only ever be one you.

Drawing Circles

Thinking back to my dancer friend Leigh's example for a moment, I could encourage other dancers to remember it's not a contest, and their performance doesn't change their worth. Those statements are true and worth exploring for anyone struggling with comparison, but there's something far more important to recognize.

As stated, we don't compare ourselves to others when we perform in a different context than they do, right? This is because we often view life in terms of spheres and circles of influence. Imagine it like this: There's a red circle painted on a floor. Inside the circle are all the dancers in the world. Since I'm not a dancer, I wouldn't be in the red circle, but perhaps in a blue one that's for streaming or an orange one for singing. Anyone who has a similar interest is in these circles with me.

I'm comfortable pointing to the red circle Leigh is in and exclaiming, "Wow, she's super awesome!" without the slightest hint of jealousy. That feels safe because she's not in my circle, and therefore we're not in competition. Neither of us is a threat to our self-worth.

But there's a bigger circle called humanity. We're in this life together and everyone has similar experiences within the same contexts. We all eat food, need sleep, have interests, go through the same emotions, use money, and give or receive care. Yet it's less tempting to compare ourselves to others in the bigger circle. We realize that an old man in Vermont has a different life than a teenage girl in California. We find it easier not to give in to jealousy because of different contextual situations, yet we all share similar experiences. So how do we stop comparing and competing as broadcasters?

Taking the top-down view of the large circle of humanity to smaller and smaller circles in which we have expertise will help us realize something vital. The more and more you drill down to a circle you're in, eventually you'll discover a circle you—and you only—fit in. No one else can exist in that circle because the circle consists of your specific context. Your history. Your family. Your hometown. Your talents and physical abilities. As stated, there is nobody else like you in the entire world. At the risk of sounding like a clichéd self-helpy feel-good book—your context is unique to you alone. You are the smallest circle.

What this information means is that if you can recognize your own uniqueness, there won't be a need for competition.

We remain guarded and defensive when we suspect someone else runs a monopoly on the experiences and abilities specific to us, when it's just not true. Each streamer is awesome in their own way. Yes, even that guy you hate on Twitch currently. We can't have peace about what we create if we're always comparing or fighting with other people. The streamer with thousands of viewers? Again, they aren't you. Instead, do the best you can in your own circle and thrive.

What's Better Than Being the Best?

Imagine how freeing it would be to admire and respect other streamers just like you admire an athlete at the Olympics, or a master illusionist such as David Copperfield? When you drop envy, jealousy, and pride and replace them with humility, compassion, and self-worth, you'll see the pure wonder of other people and their talents. You might even make connections with them, instead of being green with jealousy.

Admiration and respect will come easier, and pride will disappear bit by bit. As this process happens, you'll become free to create and connect with your audience in more ways more meaningful than being "the best" ever could.

You are wholly and uniquely you. Don't forget that. Because that's what makes you awesome and vital to this world and the community on Twitch.

CHAPTER 4 JOURNALING SECTION

1) WHAT ARE five to ten ways that you feel you're not enough? After each statement, write out why it's not true. If you need help, ask a friend to work through the list with you.

_____

_____

_____

_____

_____

_____

_____

_____

_____

. . .

2) In what ways have you moved the bar up after reaching a goal? Describe a time where you thought reaching a certain status or achievement would make you happy, but you later decided you needed more.

_____

_____

_____

_____

_____

_____

_____

_____

_____

_____

3) Describe a time where you felt jealous of someone else. Did you have a right to be? Did it make you happy? What did feelings of competition do for your relationship with them?

_____

_____

_____

_____

_____

_____

_____

_____

_____

_____

_____

4) Name a celebrity you admire and describe why.

_____

_____

_____

_____

_____

_____

_____

_____

_____

5) Draw your circles of context. These can be streaming categories, interests, friend groups, or a club. Draw at least three circles with yourself in the middle, and people you feel you compete with in the appropriate circles around you. Then draw the smallest circle around you only. How does this change the way you look at competition in your life?

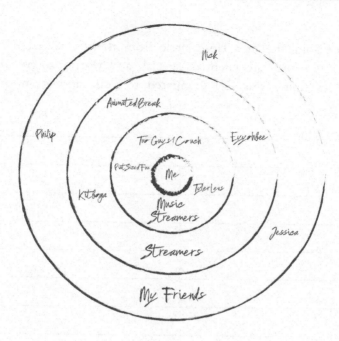

Your Circle of Context

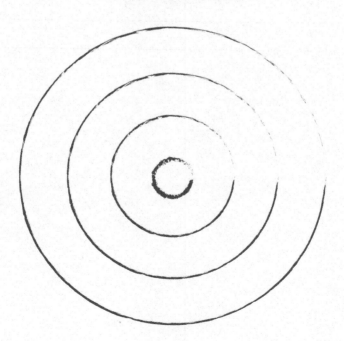

6) Name someone in a close circle from those you just drew and describe why they are talented, special, and worthy to be admired. How does doing this feel compared to your answer in question #4? Why?

_____

_____

_____

_____

_____

_____

_____

_____

_____

_____

Chapter 5

IT'S OKAY TO FEEL UNMOTIVATED

"THERE'S POOP all over the floor!" These words came from a young middle schooler named Ryan who had burst into my cabin one evening. For a few years, I was a cabin leader at a summer camp in northern Oregon.

Confused, I rose from my bunk and followed the frantic kid. Ryan led me across the yard to the boy's bathroom, and upon arrival I promptly stepped into a brown puddle. Grossed out, and looking down, I'd yet to see what awaited me. Once I rose my head, Ryan shot me a worried glance while we surveyed the damage.

I'm no doctor and don't know a lot about science, but what I think may have happened— Actually, let's go with a less disgusting visual than what I'm imagining. The last thing I want is for you to gag on the book. Instead, imagine you wanted to make chili, but took all the ingredients—beans, tomatoes, meat, onions—and flung them all over the kitchen and then stirred the ingredients with your feet. Afterward, you leave the house and hope no one saw your chili masterpiece. That visual may give you a decent idea of what I was up against that day. To say the experience was gross would be an understatement.

Ryan and I spent the next half hour mopping the bathroom, and neither of us really found out what happened that fateful evening. I can assure you though that the aftermath is seared into my mind forever. We still tell scary stories around the campfire about that bathroom.

The night of the poop apocalypse, the entire task of cleaning the bathroom seemed daunting. When you have any large task in front of you, intimidation can rule, and it's often hard to muster the motivation to do the work. This is especially true when you have a task that involves being ankle-deep in nastiness.

While your task may not be cleaning up turds, it can still be overwhelming to begin time-consuming tasks like applying for college, cleaning the garage, or shoveling a driveway full of snow. With so much effort ahead of us, it's easier not to start, which makes sense. Nobody wants to do hard stuff, because it's often a mixture of fear, frustration, and self-doubt. Other times, chores or tasks seem so huge that we're sure we'll never see the end of them. If you'll never finish, why try, right?

But what happens when the task ahead of you isn't so big? What if what intimidates you isn't just the big things, but the small, everyday responsibilities? If we truly enjoy streaming and creating, then why can it be hard to get out of bed some days? If we're chasing our dreams, shouldn't we experience some level of motivation?

Humans perpetuate this idea that if we're doing what we love, then our life should be great. We spread this odd standard as gospel truth. We believe that if we're in the right place in life, we won't have trouble with success. If we're fulfilled by our hobbies, relationships, or jobs, we won't have any problem feeling motivated.

Our culture reinforces that if we love our partner, we should love being with them 100% of the time. Or if we are in the right job, we'll be happy every day. Nothing is further from the truth.

Real trouble comes when those expectations fall short and the fallout is crushing. When we feel unmotivated, we second-guess our decisions. We decide there must be something wrong with what we're doing, how we're doing it, or even who we are. After all, if we don't love working on our dream, it must not *really* be our dream, right? We can even feel stupid or ungrateful when we're not psyched about what should make us happy.

Think about an average Twitch streamer. We play video games on the internet for fun! Some of us even get paid to do it. How awesome is that? But when you can't muster the motivation, you'll hate yourself for not being thankful. If this mindset lasts, we can convince ourselves to quit and pick up a new hobby, only to find the cycle repeating. We view trouble and hardship as signposts that things are going wrong. If there's no motivation, we must be on the wrong path. While we may feel those emotions, here's a better question to ask: Are our emotions selling us lies?

Warm Blankets of Comfort

Let's dispel this myth for a moment: It's 100% normal to not want to work on awesome things some days. In my life, I'm grateful for the amazing opportunities in my job. I work from home, stream full-time, and work next to my best friend, Dan. I even have flexible hours. Most days I'm silly; whereas, other companies wouldn't allow my offhand remarks and pranks. How sweet can things get? Yet there are days when I wake up and all I want to do is roll over and bundle myself in the covers instead of putting my feet on the floor.

Even if we love aspects of what we do, feeling unmotivated makes sense. When you get out of bed to face the day, you'll encounter hard situations and daily tasks. Some are simple, like the effort to wake up on time and shower. Others are more daunting, like calling your phone carrier to figure out why you owe them so much.

Before you get moving, you feel peaceful and safe in your cozy little bed. But you aren't the only person experiencing this resistance. As I stated in an earlier chapter, there's this idea of hustle culture where we kill ourselves by overworking. In fact, several influencers on the web even report nonstop motivation and the hustle life as if they mainline energy drinks by the gallon. However, even the greatest influencers of all time—when they're honest—have shared how they need to motivate themselves to get going in the morning.

In his journal, Roman general, philosopher, and emperor Marcus Aurelius wrote: "At dawn, when you have trouble getting out of bed, tell yourself: I have to go to work—as a human being. What do I have to complain of, if I'm going to do what I was born for—the things I was brought into the world to do? Or is this what I was created for? To huddle under the blankets and stay warm?"

We read about that freaking guy in history books and the dude ran an entire empire, yet he found some days to be a drain. His point holds true though. It's easier to stay comfortable than to start each day fresh and create new things we were born to accomplish. And after you get going, it's easy to quit when things get harder than to keep fighting. Whether what you're doing is fulfilling, it's much easier to quit and feel better now than to strive forward toward your goal.

So if you're having a hard time feeling motivated to do something, it doesn't mean you're on the wrong path, or that you should quit, or that you're foolish. That resistance means that anything good and worth doing takes work.

Kitten Punching and Motivation

A few years ago we got the cutest little kitten in the whole wide world. Orange with tiger stripes and big blue eyes. My family was ecstatic to welcome him into our home. He loved to play and had the cutest "mew" a kitten could ever produce. We named him Benjamin and fantasized about our future bliss and cuddle time with the new fur baby. But it wasn't even a couple weeks until I realized Benjamin was the worst creature currently living on earth.

Benjamin scratched everything, including my newborn son. He would hide under the couch, then wouldn't come out. He attacked your ankles as you went by. You couldn't pet him or he'd insta-flip onto his back and bite your fingers off. The demon spawn pooped everywhere but the cat box and peed ten times a day on whatever he wanted. He even sprayed the walls in our hallway.

Before you get on to me, I want to say I love animals. I know baby kittens take a while to become upstanding members of fancy cat society, as I've had several cats throughout the years. I understand how they work and like to think I'm a patient individual.

But—

I hate that stupid sack of sewer spot. He might just be the cutest thing I've ever wanted to punt into the next area code. I reached my wits' end one day when he peed on my bed right in front of me. That cute ball of fluff looked me right in the eyes and let 'er rip on my side of the bed just to watch the rage build inside of me. But that jerk knew that I wouldn't punch him into a crater, because I'm not cruel and have the heart.

But Benjamin didn't know Craigslist is a thing either.

Don't worry. He now lives with a super thankful and patient lady in the next town over. She loves him. He's pampered and fed wet cat food, while I get to never see him again. It's a win-win. All this is to say, we got Benjamin with the best intentions. Even though we thought he would bring joy into our lives, it was the opposite.

In life and streaming, there will be hard days where you get peed on and scratched and plans go awry. Your software will fail and continuing on can become frustrating. Sometimes you'll hate good things that, on the surface, were once cuddly and made you feel good. While I may have had to get rid of Benjamin for the sake of my family's sanity, this doesn't mean you should quit when things get hard or you no longer feel motivated to keep trucking, and that's the truly awful part about a lack of motivation to carry on. It can turn into shame and self-hatred.

Shame is a negative motivator we wrongly believe can cure our malaise. We beat ourselves up thinking shame will make us work harder and spark motivation, when, in reality, you feel more and more worthless. It's hard for anyone to have motivation once you feel worthless. Heaping shame on ourselves is like trying to put out a house fire with a bucket of gasoline. You can't expect the situation to get better. As shame researcher Brené Brown states: "Shame corrodes the very part of us that believes we are capable of change."

Creating Change

I'm a firm believer that in order for change to happen, you must first consider your life situations. Context in everything is the key. Here's an example of how context is important to first understand a situation.

A few years ago, our organization developed a workbook entitled *Dwarf Planet* that helps walk people through their depression and gives them practical steps toward change. But in order for men and women to find freedom, they must understand their past and present. In one example, a young man goes through a traumatic breakup and becomes depressed. His friend, with no knowledge of why he's depressed, suggests he should take some pills. The context here is key though.

He's depressed because he cheated on his girlfriend and is dealing with the moral repercussions and grief. Pills are the wrong treatment in this case, because what he really needs is a friend to listen and a big ol' dose of grace, as well as reminders that mistakes don't have to define his future. The same would be true if you went to the doctor and complained "my stomach hurts," and he told you it was cancer without ever examining you. The context is key.

When you have little to no motivation or perhaps are wondering why streaming has become difficult, then you need to dig into your own context so you can create the change necessary to combat it. If you're stressed because of an overdrawn bank account, chances are you'll have a harder time streaming and will focus on results to ensure monetary return.

If you have a problem with a close friend, you might find it difficult to stream for fear of running into them in the stream chat. Our emotions aren't little compartments that never touch each other. Instead, they overlap and get messy. Your personal life will affect your work life and vice versa. We always have to consider our situations and their context to understand why our motivation may have disappeared.

Once you understand the reason under a lack of motivation, now it's time to do something about it. It would be easy to misread this chapter and give yourself full reign to do nothing hard again. You may even look at me giving up my crazy cat as an excuse, but that's not the answer we're seeking to address in this chapter.

While it's okay to feel unmotivated, it's not okay to lie down and give up. You're worth more than that; you're meant to do incredible work that invigorates your soul and to press through those difficult moments. It would be one thing if streaming was detrimental to your health and well-being like Benjamin the asshole cat was to my family, but if you're facing a lack of motivation because of something else, here's how you can create small ripple effects to change.

Embrace the suck. We all go through lazy bouts where we lie on our couch and binge Netflix. Sometimes those moments are good for the soul, but when it becomes habitual, there's a problem. In our organization we have two military veterans who talk about how they were taught to embrace the moments that suck and press through them. It's not about ignoring that you feel lazy and stuck, but embracing the emotion, and then taking a step to break the comfort knowing full well it's not going to feel great at first. Once you take the first step toward streaming again and working through your emotions, each step gets easier.

Remind yourself of the goal, not the work. Your goal is what you're after—not the process—which is vital to remember. It may suck to go running at six in the morning, but you do it so you can stay fit, not because you love running at six in the morning. You do yardwork because you want a decent lawn, not because weeding is your favorite pastime. It's all about what you're after, not what you have to do next. Think of it this way: none of us are excited about paying a stranger $4.50 for a latte, but we do it because it's a step toward getting coffee. Always remember what you're chasing.

Make mini motivators. These are tiny, easy, and immediate rewards you can give yourself for doing a good job. If you want to redesign your website or stream panels, tell yourself that every hour you work on the website you can have a chocolate. Or if you can get the page made, you get to head to a movie. Small rewards pay off large revenues and give you something to look forward to before you reach the end goal.

Set yourself up for success. Studies show that when you prepare in advance with small actions that cut down on decision fatigue, you're more apt to succeed. This is why guys like Mark Zuckerberg and Steve Jobs wear the same outfit day after day. This doesn't mean you stay in your PJs to cut down on the decision of what to wear, but you can take little actions like setting out your next day's clothes on the bathroom counter in the evening instead of guessing what you'll wear the next day. Then set reminders on your phone to do one step toward your goal and add in the incentive I talked about.

Other examples include turning off social media alerts and putting your phone on Do Not Disturb to ensure focus instead of constant distractions. It's like the motivation version of powering up a character. Think of it like upgrades to your life.

When all else fails, cut yourself some slack and try again. You're going to have days where you feel you can conquer the world and days when it's a struggle to get out of bed. Should you feel you're slipping into old habits, give yourself a few days to slack and then create a plan to get on track the day before your slackerfest ends. Keep fighting and forging forward no matter the opposition.

Last, remember the words of Helen Keller—a blind and deaf author and activist. Many would consider her life an extreme disadvantage, yet she remained motivated and accomplished so much in her lifetime. She states, "Life is either a daring adventure or nothing."

Adventures are hard; otherwise, they wouldn't be called adventures. Streaming is one of those little adventures in life's big adventure. So you have to make a choice just like the hero of every great story does. Will you go on an adventure and face the trials it offers?

It's time to stop taking the easy way out. Instead, face the adversity offered, because that's the only way to grow. Remind yourself of your favorite heroes whether that's Luke Skywalker, Harry Potter, or Frodo Baggins. They all started somewhere and faced down intense odds, only to rise to the challenge and become the hero they were destined to be, as well as sharpening their skills along the way. They too lost motivation and wondered if the fight was worth continuing. When you feel like giving up, remind yourself what you're fighting for—and keep going.

CHAPTER 5 JOURNALING SECTION

1) DESCRIBE a time where you were unmotivated to do something fun or easy. Why didn't you want to do it? Remember, it's natural to feel unmotivated even when something should be fun. It's even more difficult to find motivation when a task is difficult or uncomfortable.

_____

_____

_____

_____

_____

_____

_____

_____

_____

_____

. . .

2) When something is hard, we can forget the reason behind why we're doing it and can be intimidated by the work itself. Remember, it's easy to feel unmotivated when you're staring at a mountain of difficulty. Instead, we need to remind ourselves that we're doing the work for a reason.

_____

_____

_____

_____

_____

_____

_____

_____

_____

_____

In what ways do you take the easy path instead of leaning into the difficult moments in life? How fulfilling is it when you do what's comfortable?

_____

_____

_____

_____

_____

_____

_____

_____

_____

_____

_____

3) What three activities or tasks do you find difficult to get motivated for? What goals are they accomplishing? How can you remind yourself of the goal instead of dreading the process?

_____

_____

_____

_____

_____

_____

_____

_____

_____

_____

_____

Chapter 6

SOME PEOPLE WON'T LIKE YOU

WHEN I WAS DATING my wife, I took her to see the movie *I Am Legend*. If you haven't seen it, the movie revolves around Will Smith's character and how he believes he's the last man on earth.

There are other people you discover, but they've turned into blood-thirsty vampire-zombie monsters. Smith's character makes his mission to save the world from a disease that turned everyone into these beasts. (My editor, Ben Sledge, wants you to know "the movie is trash, but the book is one of the best" he's ever read and even influenced Stephen King. We don't always agree on everything, especially when he's wrong.)

On our way to the movie, I remarked, "The movie won't be that scary. It's Will Smith!" We even went with some friends to a big IMAX theater eighty miles away just to see the flick. If you haven't been to an IMAX, they play films on a huge screen and crank the volume to 11. I love loud music and movies, but I go straight up old man during an IMAX film. The experience is like having a Boeing 747 crash through glass for two hours while a bunch of kids in the back of the theater drop pool cue balls on a hardwood floor.

In short, the movie was awesome, but the experience miserable. My poor, cute, innocent wife-to-be spent the entire movie in the front row with a hoodie wrapped around her face, hiding from the piercing screams and zombies with 10-foot-tall faces.

That night I learned a valuable life lesson. My wife doesn't do scary movies, even ones I think aren't *that* scary. In fact, our opinions differ often. Here are some examples of items I love and my wife detests:

- Movies about aliens, monsters, zombies, or graboids (too scary)
- Metal music (too angry)
- Rollerblading (too roll-y)
- Puffy Cheetos (too puffy)
- Yelling at strangers (too embarrassing)
- Babies

Okay, the last one is a lie. My wife likes babies, but she's not a baby person. She'd rather hang out with a toddler than a baby; whereas, I would rather hang out with a baby. After all, babies just want to be rocked back and forth and fed and take naps. Those are literally the same things I want.

But my point is that even with the person I love the most in this life, there are certain things we don't enjoy together. You will even have friends who enjoy different hobbies, music, and food. For instance, my buddy Sam doesn't like cake. CAKE! Who the heck doesn't like cake? I imagine there aren't many studies on people who don't like cake, though, but that's only because when one scientist brings it up, another scientist slaps them across the jowls like Captain Jean Luc Picard and screams, "Don't be a damn fool! Everyone likes cake! Now get back to rubbing shampoo on rats."

So while I like cake, my trusted, cherished friend seems to be an idiot in this small category of life. That's not through any fault of his though. It's just how the good Lord made him.

All this to say that while I may think cake hung the moon, and movies about zombies are dope, that's still *my* opinion. It's easy to fall into traps when espousing opinions. We wrongly assume everyone likes things we deem as good. Since the object of our affection is so good, we figure everyone reasons and values things like we do. As someone who views himself as a pretty reasonable person most of the time, when I like something, it makes sense that everyone else would too. But that's often not the case, is it?

While we know people have differing opinions, the real problems begin when we take our opinion and work it backward. Things quickly change from an opinion to a judgment call. Let's use cake as an example again. We might have an opinion like this: Everyone should like cake because it's awesome.

When we work it in reverse, however, it becomes, if cake is awesome, everyone will like it.

It's a subtle change, but the first assumes cake has value, and people should like it. However, the second hinges the value of cake on people's opinions. This reasoning gets dangerous when we do this with our self-worth or our creative endeavors. As broadcasters, we want people to watch our channel. We stream so that people can enjoy our company, creations, humor, or to connect with them. This puts pressure on us to broadcast content that people will enjoy, and can get out of hand quickly. A positive view of our self-worth changes from, Everyone should come hang out because I'm awesome! to If I'm awesome, people will want to come hang out.

We can weave a powerful lie when we change the narrative like that. The story we tell ourselves is that if everyone doesn't like me, then there's something wrong with me. If I don't have x amount of viewers, I'm not worth watching. If my content doesn't captivate each person who stops by, I need to rebrand. If viewers aren't blown away by my stream, it must be worthless. We sadly believe that if I'm entertaining —like a broadcaster should be—everyone will love my stream, and we tie our self-worth to statistics that are often based on opinions.

You Are Cake (and Other Hard Truths)

Here's a hard truth that may shatter your dreams and send you back to kindergarten or back under the covers: Not everyone will like you.

Not everyone will like you despite how amazing your personality is. No matter how funny you are, how awesome your gaming, singing, or art skills are, some people may think you suck. No matter how pretty you are, how awesome your cosplay is, or what color lights you have on your background, some people will not care. There will even be people who hate you and think you're stupid.

If you're like me, this is where you'd get all indignant. *Um, excuse me. But what the crap did I do to piss them off?* Nothing. You did nothing wrong. They just don't like you.

You are like cake to some people. Even though it defies logic to you and others, some people don't want you at their party. It's nothing personal, they just have their own opinions and interests because they're different people. Thus the lie that everyone will like us if we're awesome is exactly that: a lie.

You can't expect every single person on the planet to like you despite how awesome you are. Just like we talked about expecting perfection in our streams in the earlier chapters, we can't expect everyone's opinions or values to be the same as ours. Your awesomeness has little effect on whether people will like you anyway. Your best friends like you for who you are; hence, that's why they're your best friends. Thus, looking to how many people like you isn't a good way to judge self-worth. What you bring to this world is important because *you* are important (more on that in chapter 8).

But What If They Think I'm Boring?

When we looked at the results of our Twitch survey, we found a major fear broadcasters have is "everyone will think I'm boring." In fact, *boring* is the most commonly stated word in our open-ended fears section. Streamers are terrified of being boring. This fear makes sense.

If we're striving for an entertaining stream, new followers, subscriptions, and an active chat, we should be as un-boring as possible, right?

Welp, more bad news—some people will think you're boring. I wish I had some kind of amazing revelation that makes all this sound less horrible, but it's the truth and we all need to hear it. We'll try everything we can to convince them otherwise, but chances are, some people aren't going to be interested in what we got going on.

The good news is that having everyone like you isn't the goal to strive for. Remember, toward the beginning of the book when we talked about the goals of your stream? Go back to those. I'm willing to bet your goal isn't "to have everyone like me and think I'm the most interesting person in the world." If it is, I'd recommend doing some revisions, because it's not realistic or under your control.

Whatever you wrote for your goal, remember that that's what you're shooting for—not popularity, fame, or envy. You don't need to impress 100% of people. You just need to do your best to work toward real success. The only people you should listen to are the ones that matter in your life.

The People Who Actually Matter

Two kinds of people will show up to your stream. The first is the person who doesn't care about your stream. As stated, maybe they think you're boring or they hate your voice. Perhaps they don't like the games you play, or it's not wacky enough for them. Maybe it's too chill. For whatever reason, they don't want to watch. They may be bullies or jerks even because of issues in their life that have nothing to do with you. These are people I'll refer to as punks. Not because they're bad people, but because it's easier to shift focus off them when you say something like, "We don't worry about those punks."

The other demographic is the beaming ray of light in your universe. This group is the select lot you click with even on bad days. The jokes hit, and the memes get all the LOLs. They love the games you play and share their feelings. They celebrate alongside you and are compassionate when things are less than stellar. These people we'll refer to as huggable. The huggables show up, love your content, and want to have a great time on stream. They, alone, are the heroes of your stream and deserve a million hugs.

Because we're afraid of being boring, unliked, or failing when we stream, we try to appease the punks over the huggables. When we think of our stream audience, most times we'll change things up to attract more of the punks, instead of the people who matter. Remember that these are the people who will not engage with your content anyway, so it's insane that we continue to attempt to lure them in.

We'll try new gimmicks, new games, and every trick under the sun to attract people who may be moderately interested just to grow our audience. If by some miracle your stream grows, you will have sold out and abandoned the very people who liked the version of yourself that was most authentic and endearing. Changing yourself and the content on your stream to fit other people's interests rarely works. People are intuitive and can see through that facade easily.

So if you're doing things you don't like on stream, it's only a matter of time until you can't pretend anymore. If people do fall for the gimmicks that don't line up with who you are, they'll only be excited about the fake version of you. That entire process will feel empty and unfulfilling or will implode.

This all may sound a bit confusing—be you and don't worry about being boring—when your job on stream is to entertain people. Should you be entertaining? Absolutely. Should you do your best to make your stream not boring? Yes! But it needs to be genuine. Don't get into games you hate, genres you don't care about, or scenes you don't like. It'll feel shallow at best, and you'll be out of energy before you can even enjoy the success it may bring.

Instead, follow the advice a wise man once told me. He said his first rule of streaming is to "love the ones you're with." What that means is to love the people who show up to your stream. These are your huggables; they dig what you've got going on. If you appreciate them, they notice and you can create lifelong fans and friends. Hold on to them. Love them as best you can. Make the best stream you can for people who care. Then, when new people show up, they'll see what an awesome community you have and might stick around to have a blast too.

Imagine, then, how much more confident you'd be knowing that some people just aren't going to like you? My co-worker, Ben, is a viral writer on the writing platform, Medium, with over to 30,000 fans. He gets a lot of comments telling him what a piece of trash he is some days. When other writers ask him how he deals with that, he shrugs and says he had to learn how to have thick skin and to remember the 80/20 rule: 80% of people watching your stream will probably like it (hence, why they're watching). The other 20% will hate it and voice criticism. Most often they're the loudest, but going into a stream knowing you got 80% backing you makes you a lot more confident and it's easier to dismiss the trolls. It'll also help you pour into the people that matter.

Remember that the voices of critics often get a platform because we respond to them. Instead, let go of that craving to make everyone happy and ignore them. Love the ones you're with. And don't sweat the frustrating randos just popping in on your stream. Those punks can go somewhere where they can be more huggable.

CHAPTER 6 JOURNALING SECTION

1) WE OFTEN MAKE OPINIONS A MEASUREMENT OF our worth using reverse psychology. Instead of expecting that everyone will like us because we matter, we tell ourselves we don't matter unless everyone likes us. Use the following exercises to identify when you're swapping opinions for your intrinsic value.

Don't overthink this practice. Instead, fill in whatever comes to mind quickly and be as objective as possible. Examine not just how you feel about yourself, but how you generally think.

Your backward and unhealthy opinion:

People will _____ (love me, pay attention to me, or ?)

_____

_____

if I am _____ (pretty, nice, lovable, worthy, or ?)

_____

_____

. . .

Now let's reverse the statement. This can be difficult if you don't believe you have worth or think negative thoughts. However, I want you to try to find a word for the first blank that is positive. If you can only think negatively for the first portion, it may help to do this exercise a few times with your negative thoughts to get them on paper. Then try to move toward positive statements.

Healthy and value based opinions:

Because I am ____ (pretty, nice, lovable, worthy, or ?)

_____

_____

I sometimes expect people will ___ (love me, pay attention to me, or ?)

_____

_____

It may be a good idea to do this exercise a few times on a separate paper. There are often multiple areas in life where we swap opinion for value.

2) Name at least five tasks you're doing on your stream or in your creative life because you feel like you should or that people will like you if you do. How are they different from what you want to do? Do those projects bring you closer or push you away from your goals earlier in the book?

_____

_____

_____

_____

_____

_____

_____

_____

_____

_____

_____

3) Whose opinion do you care about? Who are the people who love you and give honest feedback in a caring way? Write their names down. Next to each, set a day and time to reach out to each one and let them know you either (A) appreciate them, (B) want to bounce ideas off them, or (C) ask for feedback. Remember, these are the people whom you should listen to—not the trolls, general populace, or your critical internal voice.

_____

_____

_____

_____

_____

_____

_____

_____

Chapter 7

YOU AREN'T PERFECT

AFTER FIDDLING FOR THIRTY MINUTES, I finally get a video feed from a third HDMI switcher. Somehow I needed a power cable that's never, ever been needed to get my PlayStation 4 to show up in OBS. Instead of pure joy at discovering the source, I'm too frustrated to celebrate. All I want to do is bash someone's face in.

To broadcast the four streams Dan and I run, we have to have a freaking crazy setup, and events like the one I just described happen often. We have one studio for all four streams and use six cameras. We often switch between three different HDMI inputs from other computers, game systems, and cameras. A while ago, we bought an audio mixer we assumed was overkill for what we needed. The device has sixteen channels, and we use almost all of them daily.

We also have five computers to ensure our streams work. Then add in nine monitors, three pairs of speakers, a wireless headphone setup, two wireless microphones, two dynamic microphones, a condenser microphone, and a couple webcams.

Why so complex you may ask? Maybe because we're clinically insane, but our current setup is the most hassle-free way to make four streams work consistently.

My point isn't that our setup is impressive, but that it's complicated. The more complex technology and streaming get, the more can go wrong. If you've ever set up a stream, you'll know that even the simplest stream can become a nightmare. Throughout everyone's day-to-day we want production to run smoothly, but then life happens. Once life happens—rest assured—things will break. A lot. Even in our daily streams, something goes wrong. A capture card won't work, a camera won't connect, the music is too loud, or our mics turn off. Problem solving gets frustrating.

Our gaming stream, The Savage Patch Kids, has been a cluster more times than I can count. We've spent entire streams troubleshooting, gone live an hour late, and had to straight cancel streams because something refused to work. The frustrating part is when everything works right up until we went live, but then hit the Start Streaming button and it burst into flames. At those moments you want to crawl under a rock and never stream again. We'd all love to have a flawless stream, but that's not the case most days, is it? It's not even the case in life most times either.

Chasing the Perfect Stream

We'd all love to be a perfect person and do our best to present ourselves in a way that declares, "I have my life together." When streaming, we want our production to run smoothly, look great, and be entertaining. There's a certain pride in that.

Anyone who comes to our stream and sees the quality knows we care, we're smart, kind, and important—kinda like that maid lady says in the movie *The Help*. Our viewers are the nice, encouraging maid lady and we're Emma Stone. If our stream goes well, we feel good. But what if the stream doesn't go well? What if our stream is more like a tumble down a staircase than a walk in the park? How do we feel then?

Sometimes I've gotten on a stream when I've already had a hard day. I assumed by spending time with an amazing community of people on the stream I'd feel better. Then my freaking camera won't show up on screen. The one event you thought would help your day get better suddenly makes the day worse. Not only that, but you feel like the viewers don't understand why you can't be more professional, and now they're judging you for your attitude.

When we've botched something we care about so much, it doesn't take long to assume our friends think we're stupid. We become convinced we're stupid. While this is true for streams, the concept is also true with finances, relationships, careers, and everything in between. In streaming and real life, we convince ourselves life should be perfect, that we should have the kinks worked out, and that failure isn't an option. Worse, we don't try new things out of fear of failure. *What if I mess this up? Embarrass myself? Or if everyone sees how bad I am at this?*

The fear of failure is a destructive thought process before, during, and after anything we set out to accomplish. We believe perfection will keep us from failure, when the notion alone is absurd. Perfection is utterly unattainable.

Failing Forward

No one is perfect. Not even you. I'm sure this concept seems simple, and you might even protest that you understand you're not perfect, but do you take it to heart? If you know you're not perfect, do you act like it? Can you treat yourself with compassion when mistakes are made? Most days we play the role of hypocrite and don't live what we know to be true. We'll even place absurd standards on ourselves that we'd never place on anyone else.

Here's a quick way to tell if you're deceiving yourself. How do you feel when you make a mistake? For example, let's say you start streaming and for the first ten minutes you're live with no face cam. No one tells you, so you assume everything's fine. Then you get a huge raid, and some jackwagon rolls into the chat and states, "Why don't you have a webcam?" Before you lay waste to his household and call him every name in the book, you open up your stream feed and realize that he's right. How would you feel about yourself?

This situation actually happened to me. I was embarrassed, frustrated, and, frankly, super mad at myself for not checking the feed. I felt like an idiot and assumed everyone else thought I was too. While I may have tried to deny it, I expected to have a 100% success rate. My belief was that if something was off, it meant I wasn't trying hard enough and was therefore stupid.

But no one gets everything correct 100% of the time, and it's unrealistic to expect perfection. Yet this is often how we treat ourselves —with unattainable and immaculate goals. By doing so, we're saying it's never okay to make a mistake. Should you put in effort? Yes. Should you do your best? Absolutely. Should you try to minimize mistakes? Sure. But know you'll mess up eventually, and that's okay because you're a human. In fact, imperfection and failure is a major path toward growth. You can't really learn most skills until you try and fail.

Michael Jordan is perhaps one of the most iconic and famous basketball players of all time. Hell, he has shoes and slogans named after him. But his most famous slogan comes from a 1990s Gatorade commercial—"Be Like Mike." Because of Jordan's success as a ballplayer, young hopefuls everywhere wanted to become the next Michael Jordan. He was unrivaled in the sport and the picture of perfection. Or was he?

Listen to what Jordan has to say about where he learned real success: "I've missed more than 9,000 shots in my career. I've lost almost 300 games. Twenty-six times, I've been trusted to take the game winning shot and missed. I've failed over and over and over again in my life. And that is why I succeed."

Failure—to one of the greatest legends of our era—was essential to growth and success. Mike wasn't perfect and failed often only to rise stronger. Every missed shot was an opportunity to learn. So what can we learn about failure from his example? Be like Mike.

Photoshopped Lives

Our online lives are fake. Photos are edited, cropped, and only taken from the right angles. Status updates revolve around what's going awesome in our lives. We all want our house to look like a Pinterest photo. But when was the last time you took a selfie crying into a pillow? Instead, most of us wear a digital mask over real life. What's even more strange is that we have apps that put an actual digital mask over our face. Have you ever stopped to think how strange that is? We want to connect with people, but literally from behind a mask.

The refreshing part about live streaming is the ability to take down some of that facade. You can edit and perfect a YouTube video, but when you're live, you're live. If you mess up, sing the wrong note, sneeze snot all over the camera, choke on your soda, or show your recent search for "How to de-skunk a backpack," it's on the internet for everyone to see.

Even if you try to pretend to have it all together on live stream, there's a point when your viewers will notice you're faking it. Your regular viewers know when you're not yourself. Yet we still want to present a perfect stream despite the inability to pull the wool over people's eyes. The fear remains that if all doesn't go according to plan, our viewers will hate us and leave.

The good news is that viewers don't want perfection—they want you to be real. That's part of the problem though, isn't it? The real you can be really messy, but that's also the silver lining. When you mess up, it show viewers you're a human being with actual feelings and problems. That's super relatable to everyone else who is tired of putting up a facade.

When you're tempted to put up the facade and act perfect, remember the wise words of Brené Brown from her book *Daring Greatly: How the Courage to Be Vulnerable Transforms the Way We Live, Love, Parent, and Lead*: "When we spend our lives waiting until we're perfect or bulletproof before we walk into the arena, we ultimately sacrifice relationships and opportunities that may not be recoverable, we squander our precious time, and we turn our backs on our gifts, those unique contributions that only we can make."

Well said, right? If we are to live connected in our relationships, we must expect imperfection. That doesn't mean we should aim for failure, but that we need to remind ourselves it happens once in a while. Even the stuff you're great at will have a hiccup or two (or three). Luckily, no one is performing brain surgery on a stream so our blunders are even more forgiving. Do what you can to keep that perspective on stream and off stream.

For me, telling someone I might expect a slipup helps a lot. On my music stream, I'll often say something like, "I'm gonna derp through this a couple times. We'll get there, eventually." Statements like the one I made take the expectation of getting it perfect the first time and allows me to experiment, fail, and improve.

Another tip to help overcome perfection is to laugh at yourself when things go wrong. We've all had that moment where we do something embarrassing. Perhaps we trip and fall in front of everyone. Maybe we spill our coffee while trying to be serious. I become enraged when I step on my headphone cable and jerk the headset off my ears. I feel like an idiot who would rather stomp those headphones down to where the mole people live than to keep streaming like everything's fine.

So what do I do despite my anger? I laugh about it with the people on my chat, then ask them what makes them rage. With the situation defused, I'm able to move on and everyone can relate, which makes me feel better.

Finally, if you want to avoid perfection, promote honesty on your stream. Some of the best streams we've ever had on HeartSupport have happened when we cancel what we're doing and talk about why we're frustrated, angry, or anxious.

Sometimes I don't want to hit the Start Streaming button. I'd rather curl up in bed and sleep until next week. But rather than doing that,

I'll go live anyway and talk about how I feel. Countless times this has opened up amazing conversations with viewers who feel the same way.

Vulnerability is one of the most powerful displays of strength. Think about a time when someone's opened up about something they're struggling with. Did you feel they were weak? Probably not. Vulnerability and honesty don't display our weakness for the world to see. Instead, these qualities strengthen our inner being and that of the viewers.

So the next time you're tempted to be perfect on stream, remember the gift of imperfection that will lend courage to your viewers and strengthen you as well. Not only will your stream be better for it, but in your day-to-day life you'll discover the strength behind the cracks in your armor.

After all, cracks are how the light gets in.

CHAPTER 7 JOURNALING SECTION

1) WRITE a list of at least ten ways you're afraid of failing on a stream or in life.

_____

_____

_____

_____

_____

_____

_____

_____

_____

_____

. . .

2) Look at your list from question #1. Would any of these be a reason you'd think less of someone else if it happened? Chances are, none of them would be an earth-shattering problem as far as loving that person. Is there any factor that makes you feel like you don't deserve that same grace and patience? Explain.

_____

_____

_____

_____

_____

_____

_____

_____

_____

3) What are three ways you can be more open and vulnerable about being imperfect? How can you create a culture on your stream that makes it okay to fail?

_____

_____

_____

_____

_____

Chapter 8

YOU MATTER, NOT YOUR STREAM

FACT: 64% of Twitch broadcasters surveyed said they feel worthless at least once a month.

I'VE NEVER UNDERSTOOD why Ultimate Frisbee is labeled "ultimate." It's like Frisbee, but I guess somehow more ultimate, and no one is certain why. I think thousands of years ago some bro was like, "Dude, let's play Frisbee. No, let's play soccer with a Frisbee! YES! That would be the ultimate." Then they high fived each other.

However Ultimate Frisbee came about, the game was a personal favorite among my high school friends. Most days after school, we'd head to the soccer field and pick teams. There were always the kids who were really into the game. They were the ones who ordered special disks online with certain weight balance and texture. I, however, wasn't that into the sport. Instead, I liked to hang out and be a part of the group.

Even though I wasn't really into the game, when picking teams, I wasn't picked last because I'm almost six feet tall. Everyone assumes you're great at Ultimate Frisbee if you're tall, but that wasn't the case. Each day there was a kid who could throw far, a kid who could run fast, and a few others amazing at catching.

Whenever a new kid joined the game and was a team captain, though, they'd pick me because I was tall. I'd joke and tell them, "Okay. But just so you know, I can't run, catch, or throw," which was mostly true. I can't run long distances because I have a heart condition that makes me tired in about ten seconds. Nor could I throw far, and I was a decent catcher at best. But I was tall! And that got me picked. No one cared. We all just liked to play. In fact, the guy who organized the game was generally a poor player (imagine Jack Black playing Ultimate and you'll have an accurate visual).

Despite the low level of competition, I still felt like I had to be a great player. But that was a false narrative I told myself. The guys I played with cared more that I wanted to include myself regardless of skill level. They saw me as worthy of their time and attention even if I missed a catch or threw the disk into traffic.

We tend to focus on performance as the marker of how much we matter. We feel the better we are at something, the more valuable we are as a person, which goes back to our chapter on having to be the best. We take our worth—both important and complex—and boil it down to how well we perform. The more we have to offer, we believe, the more valuable we are, and Twitch broadcasters are some of the worst offenders.

If we don't have a great stream, we feel worthless. If we don't have the audience we expected, we're awful. If we can't stream today, we should quit. While I covered the craving to be perfect in previous chapters, this mentality goes beyond that. We can take something we *do*—like streaming, our job performance, likes on Twitter, or the size of our paycheck—and make it the beginning and end of our value as a human being.

Basing Our Worth on the Wrong Measurement

If you place any aspect of your importance on what you create or contribute to the world, you'll feel worthless on a regular basis. This is a mental shame mechanism we fall prey to. If we examine the reality of our situation, we'll realize this is silly. Are you less of a person because your stream crashed? Are you loved any less because you forgot to turn on your mic? Does your value hinge on whether you do a good job?

A helpful way to change this negative mindset is to swap out the characters in your mental battle. Imagine your son or daughter trying to draw a house. Instead of drawing a chimney on the building, they draw a circle. Would you belittle them or tell them they're worthless? No. That's abusive and absurd. Yet this is how we berate ourselves when we base our worth on what we accomplish.

Chances are, you don't even notice you're doing this. It's a subtle lie we tell ourselves that cuts to the core of our being and builds up over time. You'll mess up, feel embarrassed, and chastise yourself. After a few mistakes and reinforced mental lashings, these cuts pile up, and with time we believe we are stupid. We'll then look at life from that perspective. Thus, any time we make a mistake, we'll harp on the blunder and reiterate a mindset that says, "See. I knew I was stupid."

This destructive perspective is harmful not just to our streams, but to our relationships, motivations, and entire life. It breaks us down until we feel we can't do anything right and become tempted to quit. Our value strictly becomes performance based, and we are not judged on who we are as a human being that's worthy of love and belonging.

It's tempting to assign our worth to what we accomplish. It's why we see so many people striving for that new promotion. If we can hit that next level, then we can prove our worth. In the case of desiring a significant other, we believe we're bulletproof from feeling unlovable. If we have a great job, no one can say we're not useful or a contributing member of society. With enough money, we assume any problem is fixable. Or if we have a nice house, we've carved out a place in the world, signaling responsibility.

Assigning our worth in this manner feels like it puts a rational status on something that, in reality, isn't easy to define. For instance, if you asked five different people the question, "Do I matter?" they may have several reasons for why they feel you carry value in the friendship. One person may believe it's simply because you're human; whereas, another believes it's your compassion that makes a difference. Because we don't like ambiguous answers, we attach our worth to things we can grasp like money, status, relationships, power, or influence.

At HeartSupport we have a saying we drive home often: "You're valuable because you're a human being, and *all* humans are valuable." Depending on your world view, this statement could be easy to accept or difficult. Think about it logically for a moment though. Why do humans feel frustration at injustice? Why do we get angry when someone we love gets hurt? Why do we cry when a friend dies?

There is a subconscious undercurrent we each have that understands the value of human life. We don't bat an eye when we kill ants, mosquitos, or wasps, but to harm a child? Even the most mentally handicapped man or woman holds more intrinsic value than the Triple Crown—winning horse Secretariat. Though we can't empirically prove that, deep down we know it's true. We all have a basic understanding that a human life means something. Men and women carry inherent value regardless of their status, salary, race, gender, age, or actions.

Thus, if it's true that humans are valuable, that means you are valuable. Period. What this means with regard to your stream is that whether you explode onto the scene and snag 60,000 followers or stick with 50 doesn't define your value. At all.

Most of us know this in our head, but we don't feel it with our heart. Though we try to convince ourselves that it doesn't matter how well our creative endeavors end up, we feel they do. Instead, we add caveats. We'll believe our actions don't define our worth in one breath, but with the other we wonder why we haven't gotten better and assume something is wrong with us. Everyone looks at themselves as the exception and not the rule.

I know my stream doesn't determine how loved I am or my importance in this world, but after a frustrating stream I, too, can feel worthless. This cycle is a broken one that only leads to more negative reinforcement. Often, however, we can confuse the times where we have an opportunity to grow with feeling worthless.

Even Manure Helps Plants Grow

A lot of kids pee their pants even after they've been potty trained. They held it too long or drank too much water. Whatever the reason, it happens. As adults, it's even worse. Even as grownups that consistently rock the bathroom stuff, we may crap our pants at some point, especially if we get hit with a stomach bug. I bet you can think back to a time when—either as a child or adult—this happened.

There's the natural embarrassment of losing control of your body functions, but sometimes we feel something far worse: shame. We feel ashamed that it happened in public, in front of friends, or happened at all. Whether it's a potty-related accident or anything else we regret, we sometimes tie the action to our self-worth, when it was nothing more than an accident or a mistake.

Shame is a concept you'll hear about often in the mental health world, but many people confuse shame with guilt. Guilt is a driving force that reminds us we screwed up or made a mistake. Guilt can be healthy because it reminds us a particular action isn't who we want to be. Therefore, we can take steps to correct the error. Shame, on the other hand, is a message that tells us because we screwed up, we are a screw-up. It's a message that focuses on our core beliefs about ourselves; whereas, guilt focuses on our behavior. Defined as such, guilt can often be a tool that brings about growth and maturity. Shame is almost always destructive.

I know I've hammered away on some Brené Brown's studies already, but remember that most of what streamers have reiterated is their struggle with worthlessness, which correlates directly to shame. As one of the foremost researchers on guilt and shame, her information is vital in explaining the difference between the two. Listen to what she states in one of her famed TED Talks:

> There's a huge difference between shame and guilt. And here's what you need to know. Shame is highly, highly correlated with addiction, depression, violence, aggression, bullying, suicide, eating disorders. And here's what you even need to know more. Guilt is inversely

correlated with those things. The ability to hold something we've done or failed to do up against who we want to be is incredibly adaptive. It's uncomfortable, but it's adaptive.

What Dr. Brown means is that when we focus on shame messages, it can lead to huge mental health issues. As stated, many streamers feel worthless. Why? Because they directly correlate their value with their performance on Twitch, thus enforcing a shame message when they fall short or screw up. Instead of taking the punches in stride and learning, we attack the very core of who we are with messages reinforcing we're worthless because we think our stream—or actions on stream—are worthless.

But guilt can propel us to new heights and help us grow as a person. Like Dr. Brown said, it tends to be uncomfortable and pits us against who we want to be. Let's say you snapped at someone on stream and get called out by your viewers. You have the opportunity to either face the music and apologize, choosing to view it as a mistake and grow. Or you can beat yourself up over the slipup for weeks on end, working harder to become a people pleaser and living in a perpetual state of anxiety.

One action will force you to confront yourself in humility, and the other will bombard you with messages about your self-worth. It's important to remember that plants grow best in fertile soil, and often that soil has manure mixed with it. It may not always smell great, and is somewhat gross, but by spreading the crap around and using it as an advantage, plants grow. The same is true of human beings. To grow, we must take our crappy actions and use them to create fertile soil and mature into the best version of ourselves.

Priority and Perspective Shifts

Where do you currently find your self-worth? Is it separate from your stream? Do you base your personal value on how well you stream and your impact on Twitch? Is your self-worth based on your social presence and how many followers, likes, hearts, or retweets you receive? Maybe it's focused around your appearance, job, number of friends, or clothes you wear. If it's based on anything other than your being a human being worthy of love and belonging, then it might be time for a priority shift.

This process isn't easy, and I'm not even going to pretend it is. Each person's daily activities, history, family, and a whole lot of other factors will play into how we view our self-worth. For some, the shift needed may be as simple as writing a list of our talents and activities, then going through them and crossing them off one by one. That simple act might help remind us our worth isn't attached to what we do. For others, the needed shift may come in the form of counseling. However long it takes, I can promise you this, it's worth the work.

If you've never thought about your worth, then talk with someone you trust and explore where you find your value. If you stripped everything you do away from your life, do you believe your life has meaning? This question will take some major soul searching. Write your thoughts in a journal, listen to TED Talks, talk to a friend or life coach, read philosophy, or sit down with a pastor. Engage your body, mind, and soul, because if you don't replace your value with something that speaks peace to your inner being, you'll continue to struggle.

There's a parable that Chinese philosopher Chuang Tzu is said to have told to two diplomats when asked to serve as a court official, and it's relevant to how we view ourselves as broadcasters. When asked for his response he said to the men: "I am told there is a sacred tortoise offered and canonized three thousand years ago, venerated by the prince, wrapped in silk, and in a precious shrine on an altar in the temple. What do you think? Is it better to give up one's life and leave a sacred shell as an object of cult in a cloud of incense for three thousand years? Or to live as a plain turtle dragging its tail in the mud?"

Tzu realized that he didn't need to prove himself by holding an important title. He saw that serving as a court official may have made him look great, but it wouldn't fulfill him. All the allure of being someone important may seem beautiful, but it's not the source of your value. You're just as valuable being a regular old tortoise crawling through the mud as one that's all dolled up and fancy on an altar. The difference is that when you realize that a high position doesn't make you feel alive in itself, you can find true beauty even in the mud.

When you're constantly worried about your image, you'll sacrifice your life on an altar of appearance for your viewers, prominently on display, and yet find nothing but death. Every stream that doesn't stroke our ego will reaffirm the banging chorus of voices in our head that reaffirms we're not enough. If a priority and perspective shift doesn't take place, then we'll continue to feel that our stream makes us worthy, and like Tzu shows, that's a death sentence.

CHAPTER 8 JOURNALING SECTION

1) WRITE three reasons you matter and are valuable. If you can't think of any reasons, ask a friend.

_____

_____

_____

_____

_____

_____

_____

_____

_____

_____

· · ·

2) For each reason you list, explain how your view would change if your stream or creative outlet wasn't successful? If it wouldn't change at all, explain why.

_____

_____

_____

_____

_____

_____

_____

_____

3) List at least three factors in your life that you wrongly hinge your worth on. That could be anything from money, relationships, job, status, likes, or follows. Try not to choose anything that's an answer from question #1. Explain why your answers from question #1 matter more than what you've listed here in question #3.

_____

_____

_____

_____

_____

_____

_____

_____

_____

_____

_____

_____

_____

_____

_____

_____

_____

_____

_____

_____

_____

_____

_____

_____

_____

_____

_____

_____

Chapter 9

TRUE GROWTH

My boss stood outside my plastic-sheeted office peeking in the door. I was two hours into what should have been a thirty-minute paint job when he finally remarked, "Oh, god. You have no clue how to paint."

Tired, hangry, and standing with a half-empty can of cheap interior paint, I turned with rage in my eyes. It was time to lay waste to his face after such a snide statement. I wasn't in the mood for teasing, and I just wanted to finish the paint job and go eat something. For whatever reason, though, I latched onto whatever patience I had left, took a deep breath, and handed the boss man my paint roller.

"Okay. Maybe you're right. How 'bout you show me how to paint?"

My boss then took a few minutes to show me a way to paint with a roller that changed my world. The process took a third of the time, looked smooth, and was easy. I'd been doing it the hard way for years and didn't even know. His example was like revealing some kind of superpower. I was PaintMan! And I had the power to paint an entire room in fifteen minutes. Since that day, I've used the method he taught me.

Even though I didn't want to hear I was painting poorly—especially because of his smart-alecky tone—my boss was right. While the advice was not presented in the kindest manner, he still wanted to impart wisdom that would improve my life. The only thing I had to do was swallow my pride, admit that I might not have it figured out, and accept some help.

In life, it's uncomfortable to accept negative feedback because it gut punches the voice that tells us we should have it together. Admitting we're wrong and making changes takes courage. As stated in previous chapters, when we feel we don't have everything together, the shame can swallow us and feed us lies. Because it's painful to acknowledge our mistakes and failures, we would much rather ignore them. We often keep pushing and never admit that we might just be doing something the wrong way.

As we've worked through this book together, we took a dive headfirst into quite the struggles the majority of broadcasters face regularly. For a quick recap, here are a few: If you're obsessed with perfection, you might be stuck in a cycle of wanting to outperform others. If you beat yourself up because of a lack of motivation, you might second-guess if it's worth getting to the next rung of the streaming ladder.

Throughout the book, you may have even seen yourself in some examples. It's a humbling experience to discover your imperfections, but then what, right? Perhaps that's what you've wondered throughout this book—why address issues I have? Do we just leave it at that? No. Just like my boss, we've discussed these struggles because they build strength when you learn to confront them.

All Aboard the FailBoat and StruggleBus

First, let's remember that everyone struggles. Human beings are imperfect and are a mash-up of experiences, values, emotions, relationships, courage, and fears. Besides our experiences and emotions, we interact with other people who have unique experiences. It's hard to imagine anyone who doesn't have a hard time throughout their life. In fact, we often doubt someone when they state life is going great and they have no problems. That's because we know how messy our lives are, so meeting someone who appears to have it together triggers our BS radars.

Why is this good news—as opposed to depressing? Because you're a human, too, and therefore are in the same lifeboat as everyone else. Even Jesus Christ reminded his followers that "in this life, you'll have trouble."

Once we realize everyone has difficulties, this opens a door to become vulnerable. When we let others in to experience our hurts, hang-ups, and imperfections, this allows them to love us for who we are—not for whom we pretend to be. Experiencing this acceptance uncovers the revelation we're not alone in what we go through.

A word I like to use to explain this concept is *grace*. Grace is empathy and care despite our failures and flaws. When we offer grace to others and ourselves, it helps us accept the things we can't change and turns our destructive shame narrative into one of conviction and growth.

I spent a season of my life learning how to write code. If you've ever written code, you'll know it's a strange art in which only insane people partake. You have to get every single detail correct or crap breaks.

In my case, I spent two weeks trying to get one tiny formula to do what I wanted. All I wanted was to make a button change color when I clicked it. Coding isn't like in the movies where you bash a keyboard and chug coffee for a few minutes to hack a mainframe. It's more like chucking your mouse pad out your window and causing a minor traffic accident while bashing your head against your monitor until a stupid button turns green when you click it.

If someone's good at coding, it's because they've spent 90% of their time the last few years flipping tables. The point being that to get good at anything, you have to experience heartache, failure, imperfection, and a whole helluva lot of grace for yourself.

Remember that successful people have generally tried and failed more times than they've succeeded, which means failure can be a good thing. If they quit everything they tried after failing, they wouldn't be where they are today. Elon Musk, the CEO of SpaceX and Tesla, has this to say about failure: "Failure is an option here. If things are not failing, you are not innovating enough."

Even though he has that philosophy on failing, nobody in their right mind would consider Elon Musk a failure. If you do, maybe you should talk it over with him in his spaceship—while in space. Musk has taken the lessons failure taught him and used those lessons to get better at what he does and now leads the industry on some of the coolest tech on—and off—our planet.

If you try and fail at something, especially something you care about, it's not necessarily an indicator you're on the wrong path. Even if you fell into a depression from the resulting failure, it doesn't mean you're a failure. Remember, we all struggle.

Instead, you did something that's stretching you beyond what you can do right now. And guess what? If you keep pushing, soon you'll level up and get even better. Then you can fail at the next hardest thing until you level up again. This, my friends, is what we call growth. Or as we at HeartSupport like to call it when life gets really difficult, posttraumatic growth.

Posttraumatic Growth

Facing adversity, hardship, and failure probably sounds good in theory, right? Head toward the fire and thrive? Smack the hornet's nest and bounce back? If this were the case, some of us would run through fields of hypodermic needles in hopes that we might get a million-dollar book deal after streaming about what we learned. But how each of us handles failure and hardship varies.

A team member once shared some personal research about suffering that depicts why we don't all bounce back. At HeartSupport, we call the findings the bell curve of adversity. The bell curves works like this. When adversity strikes, it typically affects people in one of three ways:

1. They fall apart and never recover.
2. They recover, and life returns to normal.

3. Some catapult to new heights.

Those who catapult to new heights are the ones who make the conscious decision to learn from their pain/failure/suffering and push forward. When reviewing this book, a fellow friend and streamer— Lobrowatch—made an important note. He reminded me that because of the hardship and failure he experienced from streaming, he gained confidence. But first, he had to choose to keep growing and facing the obstacles thrown in his way. That decision helped catapult him to new heights.

Some Tough Love and Practical Self-Care

If you plan on being a streamer (and human being), then it's time to act like it and lean into these adverse situations we each face. What that means is caring for yourself *and* tackling responsibilities so you can continue to grow and stream. If you're nodding your head in agreement and know you want to get serious, then the first thing to remember is active self-care.

Self-care is easy for most of us to place at the bottom of our priorities. The urge to keep going and never take care of ourselves is sometimes the biggest killer of our ability to keep going. When we say we don't have time to rest because there's too much to do, a crash is inevitable. We conclude that to get projects done, we need to work harder, Instead, we need to set ourselves up to work well.

Imagine you're going on a road trip. You only have a few hours to get where you're going. Once on the highway, you discover the tank's only half full of gas. When the gas light comes on, you continue to drive into the night without worrying because you tell yourself you don't have time to stop right now. Self-care is often like this example. We run out of gas knowing full well our tank is on empty, yet we keep pushing until the engine quits or we crash and burn. It would be stupid to go on a trip without filling the car up, yet we all do this with self-care.

To be functional, humans need a few basic necessities. It doesn't matter whether you run a business, make videos, stream, or do anything else for a living, each of us needs to fill up our proverbial tanks to keep going. Here's a short list of some benefits you get from simple tasks that everyone needs to complete in life, along with ammo to fight excuses. If you want to be a good broadcaster, these should be at the top of your to-do list.

Eat the Foods.

Like cars, human beings run on fuel, except our fuel is food. You need to eat during the day, and not just junk food and snacks, but nourishing meals. Many people today feel they're too stressed or busy to stop and eat a meal.

I, too, justify this action. Left to my own devices, I'll work all day and then around 8:00 p.m. look at the clock and mutter, "Oh, yeah. I should do that eating thing." But by that point, it's too late. You'll just look around for the easiest snack to munch on because you're starving, which is usually Doritos or a box of Hot Pockets.

This is where planning is a superb idea. Write a menu for yourself. It's one of those tasks that feels dumb to take seriously, but it's important. And we're talking about crushing important things. If you're pressed for time all day, you need to take responsibility and get some food ready the night before. We've seen far too many eating disorders within our organization justified by a busy schedule.

Planning your meals doesn't require your putting together a crazy recipe. Sandwiches are easy—bread, mayo, meat, cheese, mayo, bread. If you're not into that, then make a salad. It's lettuce in a bowl with a delicious sauce (and some protein if you want). Wanna eat somewhat healthy? Do what I do and go to Café Yumm! and snag their sauce because it's good on anything. Pick a healthy food from your house. Put the Yumm! sauce on it, and voila. Amazing!

It's simple to make the excuse you don't have the time to eat because you broadcast all over the world at the speed of light, thus everything else should be quick. But life and good habits aren't made in a microwave. They require work and planning. You already do difficult tasks all day, so you can do this simple one.

Make a list for the week, go to the store, put your meals together before you go to bed and then eat like a normal person not on the hangry train. You don't have an excuse not to do this. You're not on the White House staff, worried about whether the Russians will launch nukes if you take a lunch break. Go eat.

Make the Sleeps

Sleep is one of the most underrated items of self-care for a creative person. We justify a lack of sleep because it feels lazy. After all, why would we spend so much time on an activity that's so unproductive? Sleep seems to be what we default to when we're out of ideas, depressed, or run out of gas, so we view it as a vice rather than virtue. Plus, staying up has always been the coolest.

Ever since I was a li'l Casers playing Sonic the Hedgehog, staying up way too late was the goal. Even now, my wife and I will have date nights where we stay up and watch movies all night. Staying up late is super rad.

But you know what's better? Functioning like a human being the next day. There are a ton of reasons—scientific and personal—to get more sleep. Here's one of mine: Sleep helps you think more clearly throughout the day. If I can't think well, I can't stream well, and neither can you.

We creatives need restorative sleep. That means seven or more hours each night; otherwise, we rob ourselves of innovation and insight. Don't take my word for it though. Perform a Google search on "sleep and creativity," and you'll see a ton of scholarly articles that tell you a lack of sleep impairs your ability to reason and be creative. So get that seven hours of sleep. There are still seventeen hours left to do other stuff. Make sleep a priority.

Restore Yo Self

This necessity is the most difficult. Not only does it feel lazy (like sleep), but restorative and invigorating activities feel optional when they're critical. Every person on this planet needs hobbies, activities, or silence to restore the soul. In practical terms this means doing things you enjoy or that relax you. Go on that weekend away. Get that boba tea. Sit in the kiddy pool and listen to Carly Rae Jepsen. The world's your oyster.

For my own restoration, if I don't get alone time every day, I go crazy. I need an hour to do my own thing. While I have a family I love, a job I enjoy, and amazing coworkers, I still need to dink around by myself for a bit. I need time to go on a drive and think about nothing. I need to drink a coffee and people watch. These activities help me stay grounded and appreciate life more. I can make excuses and not do them because of busyness, but without me time, I feel like I can't think because I haven't taken the break necessary to restore my soul.

If we don't make time for restoring ourselves, we'll grow tired, resentful, and frustrated that we lack restorative activities. Again, I understand the mentality that this may feel lazy. It may feel like we're just delaying tasks we should do so we can slack off. Sure, anyone can use restoration as an excuse to be irresponsible, but we all need to have some regular activities that restore us to sanity. When you take time for yourself, you'll be a better streamer and a happier person if you feel rested.

These three simple items are imperative to self-care and rights you have as a human being. No one is going to deny you food, sleep, or an inner sense of calm but yourself. Do them. Schedule them. And make them a priority.

Real Growth Begins Beyond a Stream

We Came as Romans (WCAR) is a band we all love at HeartSupport and have worked with over the years. However, in the summer of 2018, we received a text message informing us Kyle Pavone, one of the lead singers of WCAR, had passed away from an accidental overdose.

His death rocked the team as we each had spent time on Vans Warped Tour with the band.

Jake Luhrs, the founder of HeartSupport, asked us to remain silent and take some time to process and personally reach out to the other band members. Many people took to social media to express their grief and remember Kyle, wondering how the band would continue to write music while missing one of their lead singers.

When our team finally broke the silence regarding his death, Jake released a statement explaining why we'd been missing from the public outpouring. He explained that far too often we don't take time to process and grow out of tragedy and hardship. Instead, he said, "We can numb what we're feeling rather than exploring it."

The reason I bring up this story is that we've talked a lot about ideas and the difficulties of being a streamer. But if you look at this book objectively, it's about life. You'll face hardship, failure, defeat, and hurt outside of streaming. You can process that or numb it like Jake said. You can choose to do the same with your streams. Real growth won't happen on a live stream. It will happen in the everyday decisions you make about your identity, what you value, and what you believe about yourself. When you face life head on, you'll have a choice: stay stuck or move on and grow.

The beautiful part about being a broadcaster is that you'll likely have some kind of audience, which means you can be an example of growth to your stream. You can get down on yourself for every bump on the road, or you can show your community what it looks like to be brave. Instead of despair, you can courageously fight through roadblocks and trolls to emerge victorious. You can emulate what it's like to be thankful amid difficult circumstances, because it brings about strength and endurance. You can inspire your community by being honest about real-life issues, taking off the mask, and sharing your scars.

This is actually what the members of WCAR did after losing Kyle. They could have disbanded and given up. After all, how would they continue without one of their iconic voices in the band? Instead, they leaned into the pain and shared their hurt, struggles, and failure. They opened up about where they felt they let their friend down and how they'd grown stronger as a band.

As of 2019, they're still touring and released two new songs from an upcoming album. In a stroke of humble irony, they titled one song from their first album "To Move On Is to Grow."

Today, you have a choice to grow and climb to new heights. In the lyrics to the song, WCAR reminds us that when you've already started down one path, it becomes harder to make a change. You may feel that you've already started down one path and change appears impossible. But as the band rightly reminds us, if we move forward, we can persevere.

To that end, remember, to move on is to grow. So keep growing.

CHAPTER 9 JOURNALING SECTION

1) DESCRIBE a (recent) time when you experienced failure or disappointment. What was your reaction? Did you fall apart and not recover? Did you recover and return to normal life? Did the experience help you grow beyond where you were before? How can you encourage growth the next time you experience a failure?

_____

_____

_____

_____

_____

_____

_____

_____

. . .

2) Self-care is way more important than we think. Without taking care of yourself, you're like a car on a trip with no gas. What are the aspects of self-care you're neglecting? In what areas are you doing well? Message a friend and tell them how you'd like to be better at self-care and come up with a plan to keep you accountable.

_____

_____

_____

_____

_____

_____

_____

_____

_____

_____

3) What path are you walking down in life right now? Is it a direction you want to go? How can you change course and keep moving into the person you want to be?

Share your answer to question #3 in the HeartSupport Discord (https://discord.gg/heartsupport). We want to walk beside you and help one another find true growth.

_____

_____

_____

_____

ACKNOWLEDGMENTS

First, I want to thank my amazing wife for her support and encouragement. She's literally the best person I've ever met. I also want to thank my kids for putting everything in perspective, and God for loving me and believing in me no matter how many times I stumble.

Obviously this wouldn't even be a book without HeartSupport. The past few years have been the most rewarding, fulfilling, and amazing years of my life. I can't thank our staff enough. Jake Luhrs has been a constant example and inspiration. Thank you for being willing to step into what you believe and help people, even when it's hard.

To my editor Ben Sledge—your wisdom and guidance through all the crazy times as an organization, and your care for others is inspiring. I owe you a PSL too, as when I dumped this book into your lap to edit and make sense of it when we had no idea what we were getting into. Love you, bro.

Nate Hilpert, you always believe in me and are a constant source of encouragement in deep and powerful ways. Thank you for helping me get mad strategic and plan the layout of this book so that it makes any sense at all.

John Williford, you work with a fervor I've never seen. It enriches so many people's lives, and you support me in such a beautiful and honest way. Taylor Palmby, thank you for being a ray of actual sunshine. You remind me that every single day is a gift. Uncle Dave, you've shown me how to love people in ferocious ways, while helping me step into a deeper relationship with God.

None of this, however, would even be possible without my buddy Danjo sticking by my side for eons. He's the reason I'm streaming at all and is a constant inspiration. Even though I've done most of the writing, I've learned most of the lessons in this book by spending time with him.

A huge thanks is owed to all the broadcasters who support and encourage me regularly, including but not limited to 513Kernal, AnimatedBreak, AnitaBandaid, ashnichrist, Casual_H3ro, CocoConfession, DanDrumStone, DeathDragonTTV, Doc_Bizzle, DyllonKG, Eyyohbee, Faezaria, FullOfEmily, Hamsamurai, hushyluv, iYoungGun, JustinYummerz, Kitboga, Kuhneye, LadyTapioca, Lorumerth, LobroWatch, LoparPanda, MeadowFox, MorganVinHoch, MrPureInstinct, Mxiety, PintSizedFun, Richii, RyanSummers, SethDrums, SouzyLive, twoguys1couch, TylerLevsMusic, Varghon, and a ton more people who would fill up this book with several more pages were I to list them all.

ABOUT THE AUTHOR

CaseyScreamsBack lives in Oregon with his super hot wife and three beautiful children. He spends his days drinking coffee and encouraging people on the internet, making videos, playing Pokémon, screaming rawr rawr music, and streaming with his buddy Dan. He has two dogs, Kevin and Mrs. Kevin, and a cat named Backpack.

ABOUT HEARTSUPPORT

HeartSupport was created by Grammy-nominated musician Jake Luhrs of metal band August Burns Red. After seeing his fans struggling through the same issues and addictions he went through growing up, he wanted to use his platform to impact a generation.

In 2016, the organization won a Philanthropy Award in recognition of their work at the Alternative Press Music Awards. In 2017, the organization was recognized as one of the top 100 nonprofits in the world for social innovation. The team at HeartSupport often travels around the United States educating in churches, for nonprofits, and with other organizations, while weaving engaging content along with statistics to inform and train their audiences regarding issues facing today's generation.

 facebook.com/hearsupport

 twitter.com/heartsupport

instagram.com/heartsupport

DWARF PLANET

A PRACTICAL GUIDE THROUGH DEPRESSION

Depression feels like living on a distant dwarf planet. This book is your way out.

You know the feeling. You're in a cold, lifeless place, and all alone on the fringes of the solar system. Sure, you can see the sun from afar and know other people are having the time of their life, but you're stuck on this dwarf planet of an illness no one cares about.

That ends now. This book is the result of years of coaching, studying, winning, failing, and talking to hundreds of people. Coming from an organization that's been named one of the top 100 non-profits in the realm of mental health, we'll help you discover a hopeful future. Inside these pages, you'll explore new facts about your depression and navigate obstacles that stand in the way.

If you're tired of trite books that read like medical dictionaries and want authentic and vulnerable storytelling, *Dwarf Planet* is the escape pod you've been looking for. You'll complete exercises that challenge you, read stories that inspire you, and finally feel like someone understands your struggle.

Climb in. **We're going to get you off this rock.**

Made in the USA
Coppell, TX
09 January 2020

14317674R00075